Reshoring: Manufacturing is Coming Home

By Ade Asefeso MCIPS MBA

Copyright 2014 by Ade Asefeso MCIPS MBA
All rights reserved.

First Edition

ISBN-13:978-1500841294

ISBN-10:1500841293

Publisher: AA Global Sourcing Ltd
Website: http://www.aaglobalsourcing.com

Table of Contents

Disclaimer 5
Dedication 6
Chapter 1: Introduction 7
Chapter 2: How Real is Reshoring? 11
Chapter 3: Sins of Offshore Outsourcing 17
Chapter 4: The Real Cost of Offshoring 25
Chapter 5: Nearshore Instead of Reshore 29
Chapter 6 Cheap as China 31
Chapter 7: China vs. Robots 35
Chapter 8: Lean Manufacturing Helped Win Jobs Back from China 41
Chapter 9: Is Reshoring of Manufacturing a Trend or a Trickle? 45
Chapter 10: Financial Factors Driving Reshoring 49
Chapter 11: The Return of Manufacturing 55
Chapter 12: More Companies Reshoring 61
Chapter 13: Walmart is Giving Priority to U.S. Manufacturers 71
Chapter 14: Reshoring Brings Back Multiple Strategic Benefits for Companies 79
Chapter 15: Reshoring is the Latest Phenomenon 83
Chapter 16: Is UK Ready for the Return of Manufacturing? 85
Chapter 17: Reshoring is on the Rise in United Kingdom 89

Chapter 18: Made in Britain 93
Chapter 19: Bringing it All Back Home 107
Chapter 20: Technology Manufacturing is Coming Home 109
Chapter 21: Manufacturing Came Back to Northern Ireland..113
Chapter 22: Is Reshoring Good Practice or Bad? 115
Chapter 23: What to Consider When Reshoring 119
Chapter 24: How to Ensure Your Reshoring Project Won't Fail..131
Chapter 25: Conclusion 135

Disclaimer

This publication is designed to provide competent and reliable information regarding the subject matter covered. However, it is sold with the understanding that the author and publisher are not engaged in rendering professional advice. The authors and publishers specifically disclaim any liability that is incurred from the use or application of contents of this book.

If you purchased this book without a cover you should be aware that this book may have been stolen property and reported as "unsold and destroyed" to the publisher. In this case neither the author nor the publisher has received any payment for this "stripped book."

Dedication

This book is dedicated to the hundreds of thousands of incredible souls in the Western world who have weathered through the up and down of seeing their jobs moved to Asia.

To my family and friends who seems to have been sent here to teach me something about who I am supposed to be. They have nurtured me, challenged me, and even opposed me.... But at every juncture has taught me!

This book is dedicated to my lovely boys, Thomas, Michael and Karl. Teaching them to manage their finance will give them the lives they deserve. They have taught me more about life, presence, and energy management than anything I have done in my life.

Chapter 1: Introduction

What is Reshoring?

Reshoring is essentially the opposite of offshoring, it is a term used to describe the act of bringing back offshored manufacturing to a country.

A number of American and Western European companies moved their manufacturing facilities to Asia in search of lower costs; however, rising third world wages, increasing manufacturing costs offshore, and delayed design/manufacture to market times, is making many companies bring jobs back home (reshoring).

In the beginning of 2011, for the most part, most people thought that reshoring was just impossible, that there would be no reshoring to the U.S and Western Europe, that everything was going to China, manufacturing was leaving Western country and will never come back and I think the striking thing is how much that has changed in the last three years.

You went to China because it was just so cheap you couldn't help it; but if you have got the engineers and people in the U.S or Europe, and the customer base in the U.S or Europe, you did like to be close to the customer. It gives you a shorter supply chain.

This book will highlight number of reasons why manufacturing jobs are coming back to the U.S and Western Europe. There are evidence that the great migration of manufacturing offshore is beginning to reverse. In this book we look at whether offshoring or reshoring makes more business sense now and in the years ahead.

A growing body of research shows evidence; albeit mostly isolated and anecdotal evidence; that many large companies are rethinking their offshore production locations. Some United States companies such as; Caterpillar Inc., Ford Motor Co., General Motors, Nissan, NCR Corp., Yamaha and Electrolux are already bringing a portion of their manufacturing capacity back to U.S. Earlier this year, both the Boeing Co. and General Electric publicly said that they are committed to moving parts of their offshore manufacturing capabilities back to the U.S.

Two-thirds of large U.S. manufacturers have moved factories in the past two years, with the most popular destination being the U.S., according to findings published by Accenture in May 2014. The consultancy's report indicates that approximately 65 percent of senior executives surveyed have moved their manufacturing operations in the past two years, with two-fifths saying the facilities have been relocated to the U.S.

Why Reshoring Makes More Business Sense

While the move to reshore may be slow, manufacturers are starting to recognize that many factors previously used to justify offshoring have changed dramatically over the past few years and the potential cost savings are no longer so impressive.

In some cases, offshoring has negatively affected companies' competitive advantage, limiting growth and revenue. For example, nearly half of the companies we spoke to responded by citing problems encountered with cycle or delivery time, and 46 percent experienced product quality concerns as a result of offshored operations.

As the wage gap between the Western World and China shrinks, the days of cheap labour in China are waning. The cost of wages in China is on the rise at a predicted 15-20 percent annually, while U.S. and Western Europe wage rates are increasing at a much slower 2 percent clip.

Approximately 92 percent of manufacturing executives we sSpoke to said they believe that labour costs in China will continue to escalate, and 70 percent agreed that sourcing in China is more costly than it looks on paper.

Labour cost savings are just one factor driving companies to consider reshoring. To compete more effectively, U.S and Western European companies are considering shifting operations to the U.S. and Europe to improve
    a. Product quality.
    b. Ease of doing business.
    c. Proximity to customers.

Meanwhile, rising oil prices have pushed transportation costs higher, driving more companies to turn away from offshoring as the cost advantages of moving production to China and other locations become less significant.

By reallocating resources to the U.S and Europe, companies can reduce the distance to the point of sale and eventually benefit from more accessible, cheaper fuel in domestic natural gas.

Ultimately, industries are adopting a more holistic view of production by using Total Cost of Ownership (TCO). Companies that use TCO find it is cheaper and more predictable to keep manufacturing close to home. This trend is expected to reach a tipping point over the next few years, as the total landed cost gap between the Western World. and China continues to shrink, driven in part by rising wage inflation in China and continued productivity improvements in the Western World. A separate study done in May 2014, concluded that companies are considering reshoring as an option for nearly 20 percent of their offshore manufacturing capacity between 2012 and 2014.

We are predicting that by 2016 it will become cheaper to produce certain products in the U.S or Europe that are sold to American and European consumers. The products would span half a dozen industries and include everything from machinery to furniture.

Reshoring is expected to become more viable with each passing year, as the total landed cost gap of manufacturing offshore shrinks.

Chapter 2: How Real is Reshoring?

The return of globally outsourced manufacturing; may well be the key to revitalizing American industry, and shortening lengthy global supply chains.

For over a century, the United States of America, with its autos from Detroit, textiles from the Carolinas and steel from Pittsburgh, was the world's biggest manufacturer. The U.S. spawned unrivalled manufacturing giants and household names like General Motors, Ford, Boeing and Levi Strauss. 'Made in America' goods were synonymous with quality and invention.

Over the past few decades, U.S. companies steadily started to move, or "offshore," their manufacturing units overseas to take advantage of cheap labour in developing countries; most notably China and the golden age of American industry looked to have come to an end. By the end of 2010, the U.S. had relinquished its manufacturing crown to China, which now supplies one-fifth of the goods consumed worldwide.

Today, as businesses become increasingly and sometimes painfully aware of the challenges of a global supply chain, the argument for offshoring manufacturing is no longer so clear-cut. With factors ranging from rising Chinese wages to higher U.S. productivity, and a groundswell of popular projects from the Made in America Movement to the Reshoring Initiative, the days when offshoring was the default option may be over.

Big names make the move

Several companies have already made the move back to U.S. for certain types of activities, such as ECI Biotech for its diagnostic medical instruments, Whirlpool, which will now manufacture its hand mixers in a $200 million plant in Tennessee, and General Electric for its water heaters.

Perhaps most notable is retail giant Wal-Mart, which recently pledged to buy an additional $50 billion worth of domestic products over the next 10 years.

"The economics of manufacturing are changing rapidly," said Wal-Mart CEO Bill Simon at the 2013 National Retail Federation's annual BIG Show. "In previous decades, investment mainly went to Asia. Wages were low. The price of oil was low and new factories sprung up out of the ground; but today, some of those investments are nearing the end of their useful lives, and manufacturers are making decisions about where they will invest next. Meanwhile, labour costs in Asia are rising. Oil and transportation costs are high and increasingly uncertain. The equation is changing." He added that some companies are reaching the tipping point at which manufacturing abroad no longer makes sense for them.

Even Apple, whose former CEO Steve Jobs once famously told President Obama that, "those jobs aren't coming back," has now changed its tune somewhat. "In 2014 we are going to bring some production to the U.S.," Apple's CEO Tim Cook told Bloomberg Businessweek. "This doesn't mean that Apple will do it ourselves, but we will be working with people and we will be investing our money." Cook also reportedly confirmed that the new Mac would be manufactured in Texas, and would include components made in Illinois and Florida and rely on equipment produced in Kentucky and Michigan.

Doug Oberhelman, CEO of Caterpillar, which in October 2013 opened a new 850,000 square-foot-facility in Georgia to produce small track-type tractors and mini hydraulic excavators, says his company's decision to move means improved delivery times as compared to Japan, where production was based previously.

Mike Quinn, Traditional Trade Global Head at J.P. Morgan, explains the trend. "We have seen signs over the last six to 12 months that U.S. companies who source or produce products are becoming increasingly disenchanted with China because of the increased cost base, continued regulatory irregularity and the unavailability of credit. As a result, they continue to seek other sourcing opportunities. The labour cost arbitrage game which manufacturing has been playing for the last 20 years is just about at its end as various economies pick up."

A real trend

It's clear that rethinking offshoring offers many benefits. Can high-profile moves back home by household names generate enough momentum for this trend to move downstream?

If a big company says it will grow U.S. sourcing, that creates an impetus for some of their key suppliers who do not sit in the U.S. to look at establishing capacity.

As a case in point, Foxconn, the China-based manufacturer of Apple's iPhone, is reported to be considering expanding operations in the U.S. to meet demand for U.S. made components.

It's hard to say whether or not this is a snowballing trend at this point, but given the kinds of companies that are focused on this as a priority, it is certainly becoming a serious development and a serious movement in the industry.

Despite media attention, so far there is only anecdotal evidence pointing to a resurgence in U.S. manufacturing, and the trend has yet to make a dent in the statistics. We are optimistic; It's a difficult indicator to hang your hat on, but we see far fewer import letter-of-credit transactions. This reflects the move to open account, and we see a general decline in offshore sourcing. Companies may be sourcing from agents in the U.S. who have overseas manufacturing, which would be disruptive to that indicator.

It's not a crystal clear change. It's anecdotal, but we are seeing isolated incidences that may become more of a trend over the next few years assuming that suppliers, manufacturers, and large buyers are able to leverage capital markets in the U.S. to raise money, and find the resources they need to produce the products.

One thing is clear: while there are clear economic benefits to bringing manufacturing back closer to home, there are still significant barriers. Any sourcing change has a switching cost that must be overcome. There are capital hurdles, including tooling and transition costs, savings sensitivity and or uncertainty, such as with the exchange rate outlook, and the occasional need for approval from customers or regulatory agencies.

"As suppliers look to establish new manufacturing hubs or locations, they need more financing upfront on a pre-shipment or purchase order basis for work in progress, for establishment of manufacturing capability," says Conroy, who adds that "companies who take the leap can benefit from the cost of capital and the payment process efficiency associated with reshoring as well as invoicing efficiencies and workflow efficiencies."

Some manufacturing operations, to echo Steve Jobs, really are "never coming back," such as those with a high labour content that are destined for Asian markets or make sense from a scale perspective; however, as President Obama publically commits to making America a magnet for jobs and manufacturing; manufacturing jobs have increased by almost half a million over the past three years, after a decade of decline. The tide appears to be turning: a recent Deloitte poll of more than 900 predominantly U.S. based executives and managers found that 39% believe their company is likely to deploy its next manufacturing operation in the United States, compared with only 16% who cited China as the likely destination.

Today, as companies from blue-chip giants to small enterprises consider where they should establish manufacturing, they are increasingly looking less at labour costs and more through a holistic lens that blends cost concerns with the availability of capital, proximity to upstream suppliers or downstream customers, legal frameworks, and connectivity to strategy and design resources.

Chapter 3: Sins of Offshore Outsourcing

The mistakes organizations make when implementing and managing offshore and outsourcing initiatives can be understood in the context of the seven deadly sins. Offshore outsourcing, offshore development and moving jobs offshore can have significant cost reductions when adopting a fix and mix approach. This involves an analysis and improvement of operations prior to offshoring (fix), followed by a movement of specific functions offshore where appropriate (mix).

Offshoring business operations offers the potential for cost savings of 15 percent to 20 percent, but Compass analysis show that organizations that properly plan and operate offshore initiatives can reap substantially higher rewards.

Organizations that focus on short-term cost reductions often rush through projects without adequate planning, due diligence or consideration of the long-term implications of the inevitable changes in business requirements or offshore market conditions. In many respects, the mistakes organizations make when implementing and managing offshore initiatives can be understood in the context of the seven deadly sins; pride, sloth, avarice, lust/extravagance, envy, gluttony and anger.

1. Pride

Many organizations succumb to the sin of false pride and plunge headlong into an offshoring initiative without performing due diligence. They assume they have the internal capabilities to create and govern an offshore operation, but they seriously underestimate the management resources needed to set up and run such an operation. This contributes to poor productivity and communications, and to missed cost savings and improvement targets.

It takes time, good planning and detailed execution to offshore successfully. An organization unwilling to invest time at the outset and do it properly cannot expect to reap the long-term benefits of offshoring. Don't be too proud to learn from the mistakes of others, nor too arrogant to assume that you can cut corners in implementation and abdicate the responsibilities associated with the ongoing management of the operation. Acknowledge that your existing internal resources may not be adequate. Invest the time and resources needed to do it right the first time and keep it successful over the long term.

2. Sloth/Laziness

It's lazy to move an inefficient business operation offshore and rely on lower salaries to run the operation at a reduced cost. This "lift and shift" strategy is seriously flawed. Although individual salaries may be substantially lower in an offshore environment, the personnel resources required increase by as much as 15 percent.

Lift and shift strategy can achieves short-term cost savings, but does not address underlying problems. When these problems are offshored, the solution is often to throw additional resources (people) at the problem. This strategy becomes unsustainable over time as offshore salaries increase and traditional offshore locations experience staff shortages and high turnover (up to 80 percent a year in certain sectors and regions). A decrease in individual productivity is common in offshored environments. While offshoring to a captive operation offers the chance to solve problems over time, outsourcing a "lift and shift" approach means managing problems through a third party.

Top-performing companies are shaking off laziness and adopting a "fix and mix" approach. This involves an analysis and improvement of operations prior to offshoring (fix), followed by a movement of specific functions offshore where appropriate (mix). Data shows that the investment in such initiatives is more than offset over the long term by increased savings.

3. Avarice/Greed

In offshoring projects, avarice shows itself as a lack of concern for the fate of the business, as well as a disdain for the well-being of offshore development. Apart from the dubious morality involved, this approach eventually collides with the reality of staff-retention problems offshore, and the associated cost and quality problems. A long-term view focuses on investment in local resources, specifically in staff training, orientation and retention. Offering a career path will pay off in higher productivity and lower attrition.

4. Lust/Extravagance

The desire to solve a problem by taking on more, cheaper personnel is extravagant and wasteful and has serious implications for service quality. Many offshore operations have lower productivity and excessively high turnover, reducing cost savings.

Here is a typical scenario: A problem is offshored, and additional lower-cost but highly educated staff are thrown at the problem, without any effort to find a solution. After awhile, employees grow frustrated and depart for more rewarding jobs, which means more staff must be hired. A vicious cycle is created. Service quality and cycle times suffer, and error rates increase.

Upward salary pressure in India and elsewhere is forcing organizations to seek new destinations, but the low-cost/low-efficiency model will likely be replicated in those markets. Although the salary differential between onshore and offshore workers remains substantial, the combined effects of lower productivity, increasing salaries, hiring/training replacement staff and managing problems associated with continuity will close the gap far sooner than anticipated. Fixing problems before offshoring enables organizations to reap the benefits of both lower salaries and an efficient organization.

Don't give in to the impulse to compensate for low productivity with more bodies: It's a false economy. Leading organizations apply the same continuous performance improvement mind-set to offshore operations as they have applied to onshore operations for years. Companies that have invested in technology, infrastructure and processes in their offshore operation continue to show improvements in productivity and cost savings.

5. Envy

Don't succumb to envy and offshore operations because you think others are reaping huge savings. The discounts are not nearly as deep as touted. Claims of cost savings of 40 percent don't account for the impact of lower productivity offshore, higher communications costs and the additional overhead for onshore governance. Actual savings are closer to 20 percent.

Analyses of onshore operations frequently identify cost-saving opportunities of 20 percent to 25 percent, attainable through the application of technology or improvements in business processes. In other words, offshoring may not be necessary to realize cost-saving targets. Before embarking on an offshoring strategy, a firm should gauge the current and potential efficiency of its onshore operations, and the investment needed to realize the potential efficiency.

Offshoring continues to grow, but concerns over the quality of customer service are driving some operations back onshore. This trend is particularly evident in call centres involved in product advice and direct sales. Companies currently repatriating some of their services have concluded that a client-facing operation onshore (and/or a customer segmentation strategy) can offer a competitive advantage.

6. Gluttony

Some organizations succumb to gluttony and offshore as much as possible, as quickly as possible, believing this will maximize savings. But companies have a limited ability to digest change and an even smaller capacity to digest offshore change. Organizations that indulge in gluttony find their management focus will ultimately be directed toward fire fighting.

The experience of IT outsourcing offers some lessons. Early ITO deals were characterized by a soup-to-nuts mega-deal approach as a way to achieve substantial savings and value-add. Over the past few years, this strategy has failed to deliver, and selective sourcing has emerged as an alternative.

IT outsourcing worked for companies that took a measured approach, designed an optimal mix of outsourced/insourced/offshored service delivery, adopted a best-of-breed strategy regarding service provider selection and built internal governance capabilities to manage their operations.

Resist the urge to offshore everything at once. Instead, take a measured approach, process by process. Monitor success and identify what works and what the management team can handle. Build confidence and experience by gradually moving the operations. Establish a track record and develop the governance capabilities to maximize potential benefits.

7. Anger/Wrath

If a sourcing relationship goes awry, the business might be tempted to blame the outsourcer, but both parties are usually responsible for the results. Some clients mistakenly believe they can simply outsource major problems. Others have un-realistic expectations about the cost savings achievable.

If an offshore outsourcer has failed to deliver on expectations, don't get angry. Acknowledge your contribution to missed goals and objectives. Channel your energies in a positive manner, work with your outsourcing partner to discover the source of the problems and chart a path to success.

Chapter 4: The Real Cost of Offshoring

There is a growing trend to reshore manufacturing back to the U.S. and Western Europe as managers recalculate and compare the true total costs of production. Still, there is a range of hidden metrics that are not factored often enough when determining where to produce goods.

Too many companies moved their production to countries like China based solely on the unit prices. Buyers are rewarded with the money they save their company based on the piece price however they failed to see the bigger picture.

As the cost of manufacturing overseas is being re-examined using total costs models, several factors have been at the forefront. Below are the major factors that first led to bringing work back to the U.S and Europe.

1. Inventory: Businesses are being forced to buy larger lots to get the best China price.

2. Cash flow: Lower-volume businesses are being forced to pay for parts before they are shipped. Only the major companies are getting favourable terms.

3. Travel: This can chip away at savings. If travelling to Asia becomes necessary or frequent, which often happens when the qualities of parts are sub-par and the manufacturing has to be reworked.

When one or two of those problems became egregious, then companies would make the determination to return manufacturing to the U.S. or Europe.

Below are other hidden costs of sourcing production offshore.

1. **Currency Fluctuations:** Last year's invoice of $100,000 could be $140,000 today.

2. **Appropriate Management Skills:** Many companies underestimate the people, process, and technology required to manage an outsourcing contract.

3. **Design Changes:** Language barriers make it difficult to get design changes understood and implemented.

4. **Quality Problems:** Substitution of lower grade or different materials than specified is a common problem.

5. **Legal Liabilities:** Offshore vendors often refuse to participate in product warrantees or guarantees.

6. **Cost of Transition:** It is easy to overlook the time and effort required to successfully offshore production. It takes from three months to a year to complete the transition to an offshore vendor.

7. Poor Communication: Time zone differences and language barriers can make communication complex and burdensome.

8. Intellectual Property: Foreign companies, particularly Chinese firms, are notorious for infringing on IP rights without legal recourse for American and European companies.

Labour makes up about half of typical manufacturing cost. If you can drop the labour costs by 40 percent to 80 percent by moving offshore then that really impacts operating profit. What is unseen is the cost of unemployment, health care, Social Security, and all of the infrastructure costs that result from the loss of manufacturing plants.

American and European consumers are also putting more pressure on retailers to have more American/European made products. Recent polls indicate 78 to 80 percent of consumers would be willing to pay more and prefer to pay for U.S or European made goods.

Chapter 5: Nearshore Instead of Reshore

Moving operations back to the U.S. isn't for everyone. Taxation, in particular, is a pain point, as U.S. nominal corporate tax is higher than in any other country. Labour is also a worry; as it's been a generation since certain types of manufacturing left the U.S., the foundational manufacturing assets are not there and it's not always possible to find management or employees with the right skill-sets. Companies are therefore faced with the challenge of attracting and training a new generation of factory workers while also protecting their bottom lines.

Another option, then, for companies considering relocating their already offshored operations is 'nearshoring'; bringing production closer to their key markets, which for U.S. companies might mean Latin America or Canada.

Mexico is facing security issues, however this has not prevented corporate investing there. For example, we are seeing companies from the automotive sector building plants in Mexico. It's a country that is growing and the growth expectations are big. It's not just carmakers who are finding Mexico an attractive option. Since the country's sweeping energy reform, the oil and gas sector also looks set to become a hotspot for U.S. investment.

Moving to Mexico, which was once a favoured spot for many U.S. based manufacturers and has the available labour pool, also makes sense to the bottom line; manufacturing wages, adjusted for Mexico's superior worker productivity, are tipped to be 30% lower than in China by 2016. Furthermore, the country's raft of free trade agreements positions it as a hub for products for export. Investment in infrastructure such as roads in Mexico has been very high over the last five to six years, which helps suppliers. It is cheaper and faster to ship from Mexico to the U.S. than from China to the U.S. and that gives Mexico a competitive advantage against China.

Mexico also beats out Far East competition in terms of proximity to customers, reduced cultural and linguistic barriers, the strength of intellectual property protection and transport costs. In an unlikely twist, manufacturing in Mexico could also be good for the U.S. economy. Mexican factories use four times as many American-made components as their Chinese counterparts. Shorter lead times, better supply chain control and better communication are some of the benefits of nearshoring.

Mexico is open in terms of raising finance; companies can go to the commercial banking sector to access finance, they can go to the capital markets and there are also non-bank institutions that are also getting into the market. Manufacturers are looking at cost of goods sold and working capital as drivers. They are looking for better visibility, operational visibility and cost between themselves and their customers.

Chapter 6 Cheap as China

China, once the go-to option for offshoring operations, now doesn't look as attractive, and it's not just U.S. companies who think so. A recent Bloomberg report highlights that even Taiwanese manufacturing, which had migrated to mainland China because of the lower labour costs there, is now on its way back home.

A recent report calculates that annual wage and benefit increases of up to 20% at Chinese factories will slash its labour-cost advantage over low-cost American states from 55% in 2011 to 39% in 2015. When the higher productivity of U.S. workers is taken into account, this could be enough to virtually close the cost gap between the U.S.

While there are still other offshore jurisdictions offering cheap labour such as Vietnam, which with wages around half those of China, has already seen an influx of sectors such as apparel production; the unreliable delivery, transport delays, long supply chains and often unpredictable quality involved in outsourcing manufacturing to the Far East is leading companies to think twice about where they put their factories.

"Particularly for U.S. companies, the primary driver for offshoring manufacturing was cost and cost continues to be one of the drivers," explains Dave Conroy, Regional Trade Executive for North America at J.P. Morgan. "But with the landscape changing around different regions and different countries that have been focal points for offshoring, changes in their economy, the emergence of China's middle class and a high wealth class, and the strength of the renminbi as a currency, a lot of companies around the world have been given pause."

A survey in April 2012 found more than one-third of U.S. based manufacturing executives at companies with revenue greater than $1 billion planned to reshore production to the U.S. from China, or are at least considering it.

But it's no longer solely about cost; companies are now looking at the bigger picture and factoring in the associated cost of offshore manufacturing, inclusive of all the embedded costs around logistics, control, intellectual property, compliance and quality. They are also finding that bringing production closer to the point of sale means their employees can engage more directly with customers and adapt quickly to changes in the market. As Caterpillar vice-president Mary Bell said at the time of the industrial firm's move to Georgia; "the decision to shift production from Japan to the United States is driven by the proximity to a large base of customers in North America and Europe."

"Speed to the market has an inherent monetary value," adds Quinn, "such as increased revenue because you are not discounting products that are at the tail end of the season."

Changing conditions in offshore locations are not the only factor driving manufacturing back to the U.S. Rapid advances in shale gas development have led to collapsing gas prices, and this, coupled with the rise in oil prices over the past decade which sent transportation costs soaring, means that it now makes more sense to stay home. In fact, in April 2012, the U.S. National Association of Manufacturers said that additional shale gas development could create 1 million manufacturing jobs by 2025. As a result, for sectors ranging from fashion to energy-intensive industries, like chemicals and metal, the United States is an attractive place to be once again.

Chapter 7: China vs. Robots

There is a bit of a disconnect between international relations theory people and economic theory people. It is rare that a single person finds himself facile with both disciplines and this tends to introduce blind spots in thinking. One of the biggest blind spots concerns the future role of manufacturing in geopolitics. Many people believe that cheap wages in places like China will ensure a strong US-China trading relationship and reduce the chance of future security competition. They think China will rise peacefully. These people are missing an important economic trend; the decreasing relevancy of the US-China wage gap and the inevitability of "reshoring", the relocation of manufacturing back into western countries.

Here are other reasons why reshoring is happening

1. Energy Costs

The first big pressure to reshore is going to be rising energy costs. Lets have a look at crude oil prices over the last decade:

The 07-08 price spike didn't last for several reasons:
    a. The economic crisis reduced demand.
    b. Efficiency improvements reduced demand.
    c. Alternative energy (fracking, solar, nuclear, coal, wind, etc.) increased energy supplies.

d. The US government opened the strategic fuel reserve, increasing supply.

As the global economy found its legs, demand is once again rising and new supply is harder to access and costlier to drill. At a certain point, there just aren't enough available efficiency improvements to make it reasonable to send goods that are to be consumed in the US or Europe across the Pacific Ocean. Rising energy prices have begun to countervail cheap Asian wages. The global economy is decreasingly a wage game, and increasingly an energy game. While in years to come energy costs might well prove sufficient reason in themselves for companies to reshore, the pressure to come home is compounded by the possibility that manufacturing may soon no longer require large numbers of workers, which brings us to…

2. The Robot Economy

Robots are better workers than people. They are more consistent, they work more hours, and they don't unionize. America's tech companies are working every day to create the kind of computing power that eventually leads to highly efficient robot workers. The question is not if the robots will arrive, but when. When they arrive, they will eliminate any reason for companies to incur the energy expenses of offshoring.

What does that mean? It means that manufacturing in the developed world will make a dramatic jobless recovery. Energy (and consequently, transportation) will become the limiting factor in production, and that means that geography is going to matter a great deal. Businesses will attempt to locate themselves close to both consumers and their suppliers, and that means that manufacturing is going to make its home in the high-density population centres of the United States and Europe where domestic demand is highest. Countries with weaker domestic demand (i.e. developing countries) will have to import, and the high energy costs of transporting those goods will raise their prices and slow their growth rates.

This is not an outcome a country like China looks forward to, and it is for this reason that the Chinese are not just targeting growth rates, but high growth rates that border on being unsustainable. China needs to develop self-sustaining domestic demand to rival the US and Europe before the robots come if it wants to keep the new foreign businesses that have been driving its boom. Can the Chinese pull it off? Only time will tell, and the United States still maintains the leverage to help or hinder China in this respect for now.

Assuming China can't outrun the robots, how will this affect the American or European consumer? Two ways:

a. Products are going to be cheaper and higher quality. Americans and Europeans will no longer pay for the wages of foreign workers or the energy costs of shipping good across the ocean, while robots will ensure higher quality products of more consistent quality.

b. There will be no job growth produced from this, and the profits the robot companies will reap will consequently be distributed very unevenly, worsening economic inequality, weakening demand, and potentially contributing to secular stagnation.

How will we confront the demand-depressing inequality that the robots will produce? There is a mix of policy options for escaping that trap.

a. New jobs and new sectors as yet unimagined; even if this is possible, it's doubtful that low-skill workers will be able to do these jobs (if they could, why not use robots?). This forces us to drastically change the skill set of most of the workers in the economy, and this may not be possible due to natural inequalities in abilities and talents and the inability of the state to accurately predict what skills will be needed in the economy 20 years from now.

b. We can pay citizens to consume and pursue whatever projects they can think up. This means a universal basic income, and it means we embrace Russell and Keynes' views denying the value of work; however, the owners of the robots are unlikely to see that by giving up large portions of their wealth to redistribution they can actually increase their sales and wealth over time. Given that Western Countries political system relies on financial donations, the robot owners will likely buy the candidates and prevent this outcome from arising on its own.

c. Service Economy; the robot owners may attempt to pay everyone else to pamper them, as in the Gilded

Age. The masses become their servants, hence the term "service economy". The rich attempt to pacify the masses with bread and circuses. Most of the population spends their lives high on something, and we end up happy slaves. Think Brave New World!

d. Marxist Revolution; the people rise up and nationalize the robots, hanging the robot owners by the rope their robots made.

e. Political Reorganization to get the Keynesian Utopia; either by structural reform or structural reconstitution, we adjust the way the political system makes decisions in order to yield option b when it otherwise would not.

I don't think we can do option a in a reliable way, b is a pipe dream given the current system, and d has a host of issues. There's the ordinary problem with Marxist revolutions; what kind of state will rise in their wake? Will the cure be worse than the disease? On top of that, a Marxist revolution is very difficult to accomplish in a non-agrarian society with modern military capabilities. The people only beat the army when the army defects to the side of the people, and robot soldiers don't defect.

Therefore, the likely outcome is either the service economy or some kind of political reorganization in which the robot owners are politically outmanoeuvred, ideally before they get killer robots they can turn loose on the rest of us!

That is what happens on the domestic level. What about internationally? This turn of events means that the US and European economies will not always be deeply intertwined with China's, and that means that future security competition between the west and the east is more likely than is commonly perceived today.

As for what happens if the Chinese do manage to develop faster than energy prices rise or human beings develop robot workers? In that case, the same things happen, they just happen in China too. China becomes more self-sufficient economically, and the economic connection between west and east lapses, albeit not as much or as quickly.

Chapter 8: Lean Manufacturing Helped Win Jobs Back from China

You have got to be good to win back manufacturing contracts from China. Vermont Castings has succeeded in doing just that, thanks to the introduction of "lean manufacturing" principles, put in place over the past years.

The lean approach, according to the company's new general manager, has brought stunning new efficiencies not only in the production of contract cast-iron components for other companies, but also in the manufacture of Vermont Castings' trademark stoves and fireplace inserts. Vermont Casting has been able to work efficiencies into its production line, without sacrificing quality.

"It took more than competitive bids to win new contracts from the Jotul and Harmon stove companies, and other manufacturers. The cast iron from China is nowhere near the quality of what we get out of Randolph." he commented.

Lean manufacturing, is not a slash-and-burn approach to cutting costs. Rather, it is a clear-eyed analysis, by management and on-the-floor workers, of production practices from beginning to end.

It's a total re-thinking of the way we do business. Lean manufacturing is really about eliminating waste.

A major source of waste, is excessive handling of components and finished products. Handling, adds no value to a product, but plenty of labour and storage costs.

A year ago, Vermont Castings was renting warehouse space to store component parts until needed, as well as finished stoves and fireplace inserts, until they were shipped to dealers.

The foundry worked on a "batch system," producing, for example, hundreds of stove doors that all had to be handled and stored, until they were pulled for assembly.

Fast forward to today, where production is a lot more flexible and the need for storage space has shrunk to the point that Castings no longer rents warehouse space. Component stove parts are now delivered from the foundry twice a day, and they go immediately to the assembly line, where workers build one of the 15 models in the Vermont Castings line-up. The stoves and fireplace inserts then go directly to the finishing department for enamelling and other surface treatments.

Working Smarter

More flexibility at the foundry and on the production line means that Vermont Castings can turn out particular models as needed, instead of amassing months' worth of inventory.

Of course, a small inventory and quick turn-around requires a very savvy marketing arm, able to predict the demand for products. The company's marketing director, keeps tabs on several markers, including the water temperature in the Caribbean. Warmer ocean temperatures mean more hurricanes, possible disruption of Gulf of Mexico oil refineries, higher fuel costs and a surge in demand for wood-burning stoves.

Thousands of square feet of the Bethel plant that were once used for storage have been converted to more productive uses. One corner of the plant is now devoted to the production of Vermont Castings' new line of more affordable steel stoves.

A massive laser cutter used to cut sheet steel, presses to punch holes, multiple welding booths, painting stations, and more. None of this was there a year ago; no one knew about sheet metal fabrication.

Over the last year, Castings has also been able to find big savings by manufacturing at the Bethel plant items that were formerly purchased from suppliers. It's called "in-sourcing." Castings employees, for example, now fabricate from scratch the cement "refractory panels" mounted inside woodstoves to retain the heat.

Another example: In the past, Castings bought and had to store wooden skids for packing and shipping stoves. A year ago, they had skids stacked to the ceiling. Now, employees make the skids, in-house and as needed.

Management sets the direction and goals for lean manufacturing changes. For the process to yield big results, engaged workforce, willing to learn new skills and able to provide ideas for new efficiencies, is essential.

Chapter 9: Is Reshoring of Manufacturing a Trend or a Trickle?

There is a lot of buzz around the reshoring of manufacturing. I have been a bit sceptical of the buzz and decided to see if there was something to it, or if it was just wishful thinking. So I designed a survey and sent it to the senior operations managers of manufacturing companies in June 2014. The results confirmed that reshoring is indeed real, and the reasons are not the ones that would immediately come to mind.

The real eye opener for me was that 40% of the companies indicated they have won new manufacturing business this year that had been previously off-shored. I consider that to be a meaningful number and very encouraging for western manufacturing. I was intrigued and decided to drill in and uncover the motivating factors for the reshoring, and here is what I found.

1. Product companies are ordering in smaller lot sizes because they are concerned about the economy and the continuing demand for their product. As such they would rather produce in smaller quantities and not get stuck with cash tied up in inventory. These companies understand that in most cases it costs more to re-shore the work and produce in smaller quantities, but they rationalize the extra cost against risk mitigation and flexibility.

2. The digitalization of manufacturing has matured and converged. Computer Aided Design (CAD) software, Computer Numerically Controlled (CNC) machine tools and Internet based manufacturing networks have made producing complex parts and tooling akin to printing documents on network printers. This digitalization allows for distributed manufacturing such that companies can easily produce closer to their customers wherever in the world they may be versus in a single factory. By producing closer to their customers, companies save on logistics, take advantage of local economies, tweak products to local market preferences, build goodwill in the local market and mitigate the risk of a single production factory.

3. The life expectancy of products is continually shrinking. Companies need to iterate quickly to introduce new products and react to competitive pressures. Locating production near a company's engineering / marketing teams affords a collaboration that is crucial for innovation and time to market. Companies that don't want to compete by being the cheapest product are retooling their business and supply chain strategy to allow them to compete based on speed as well as innovation.

4. We have become a society that likes to customize products and experiences to our tastes, and we are willing to pay a premium for it. Starbucks is a great example of us paying a premium for customization, we could buy a coffee at the convenience store for $1 but we go to Starbucks and pay $4 for a customized coffee. This same behaviour is permeating the

product sector and companies are quickly learning that there are fat margins in allowing customers to tailor some aspect of their product to specific tastes. That business model shift does not lend itself well to producing on the other side of the world. They need to be close and nimble.

Another contributing factor, but not the primary driver of reshoring is the strong Chinese currency; Oil prices and increasing labour costs in traditional low cost countries were also cited as reasons contributing to reshoring decisions. As low cost countries develop and cost rise, there will be emerging countries with low cost labour eager to woo companies with commoditized products competing for thin margins.

Product companies and original equipment manufacturers (OEM's) are expected to protect and grow their market share in addition to making profits for their shareholders. They get rewarded by producing great products and consistently producing solid business fundamentals. They are not rewarded for patriotism. Fortunately for certain western manufacturing sectors, reshoring does make for a sound business decision when all factors are considered. Don't get me wrong, we have a positive trend for the right reasons, not a gold rush, but I'm happy with a positive trend when it comes to manufacturing in the west.

Chapter 10: Financial Factors Driving Reshoring

There is no question, as more and more stories about the reshoring movement bubble up to mainstream news, that the state of global manufacturing is in flux and that long-held assumptions about the costs and expenses in manufacturing should no longer be considered accurate. Due to a variety of factors including cost and availability of materials, climate change, and disputes on the rights of workers, American manufacturing may soon be a far more American enterprise than it once was. In fact, the US has now surpassed all countries but Mexico, India, and the Netherlands in cost savings potential for manufacturers.

Several years ago, President Obama is reported to have asked Steve Jobs what it would take to bring lost manufacturing jobs back to America. Steve Jobs is said to have responded that there was no way that those jobs were ever coming back. At the time, Jobs's assertion was based on good evidence: it had long been more economically efficient to outsource manufacturing to other countries, and there was no indication that that would change. Now, due to factors that Jobs would have been unable to foresee, manufacturing now looks very different from what it was just a decade ago.

1. The changing status and laws on labour in other countries has drastically impacted the costs

of exporting labour, adding to the reshoring movement.

In past years, China offered significant savings over American factories because labour in China was so much less expensive; however, since 2005, wages grew at a much higher rate for Chinese jobs than for American jobs. Over the course of the last decade, this along with the growing value of the Yuan has led to an increase in manufacturing costs in China of 187% compared to an increase of only 27% for the cost of American manufacturing. Throughout the rest of Asia, wages increased by an average of 7.1-7.8% between the years 2000 and 2008. As a result, wages throughout Asian markets now nearly match American wages as the market crisis actually produced a drop in average wages for factory employees by 2.2% since 2005.

2. Affordable options in automation even out the playing field among American manufacturers.

Recently, Bill Gates noted that the proposal to increase American minimum wage would likely cause many manufacturers to rely more heavily on automation. As wages likewise rise in other countries, manufacturers turning away from offshoring and joining the reshoring movement can find significant cost savings by investing in automation and in terms of productivity, investing in automation saves manufacturers money within the first year as a single machine can increase productivity by as much as 70% while only costing as much as a single employee's salary for one year. Regardless of the concern that automation costs jobs, the savings potential of the technology nearly necessitates that manufacturers consider it as a valid option. This trend of "botsourcing" has already made some major impacts on the world of manufacturing: Foxconn recently announced their intent to join the reshoring movement by investing $40 million on a largely automated facility in Pennsylvania, while Amazon recently spent $755 million to purchase Kiva Systems, a manufacturer of warehouse robots.

3. Environmental standards and energy costs change the expectations placed on manufacturers.

Because of the new availability of shale in America after 2005, it has become cheaper for American manufacturers to depend on energy produced at home. According to the most recent PwC report, as many as 87% of CEOs in industrial manufacturing consider the environmental impact of their operations to be a point of major concern, while 70% also stated that volatile energy costs represented a serious issue. While in some ways, this simultaneous interest in cheap energy as well as environmental protection is contradictory, each of these inclinations would make manufacturing at home in the US a better choice, literally fuelling a large portion of the reshoring movement.

Locally produced energy has become cheaper and so manufacturers can eliminate the environmental cost of transporting goods overseas. In addition, in the US manufacturers face more stringent requirements from the Environmental Protection Agency, which means that operations performed at home are more likely to correspond to accept regulatory measures. While in the past these strict requirements may have led some manufacturers to move labour overseas, the increasing number of manufacturers who are aware of the importance of curtailing the environmental impact of their operations may mean that they are less deterred by the requirements of the EPA to keep operations in the US.

4. Lacking regulations on intellectual property rights and on worker safety impact how American manufacturers invest.

After last year's Savar factory collapse, many consumers and legislators called for improvements in working conditions and safety regulations for workers in factories supporting outsourced American operations. While some manufacturers continue to resist legislative intervention in their safety regulations, many manufacturers were motivated to change the ways in which they select factories and materials providers. Similarly, as many as 58% of manufacturers say that the lack of enforcement of intellectual property rights in China and other countries is a major detractor for doing business in those countries. For both American consumers and manufacturers, lack of enforcement of these kinds of regulations are often seen as unacceptable, and like most great social causes which started in movements by doing good, so is the reshoring movement.

5. Both consumer and supplier opinions are evolving:

According to marketers today, customers are now likely to express a greater interest in purchasing goods that were made locally, by hand, on a smaller scale, with lower environmental costs, and in ways that are more sustainable for the American worker. In fact, as many as 80% of consumers say they would pay extra for goods made in America. Whether or not some may find these ideas too trendy or reliant on buzzwords, many manufacturers are paying attention. In fact, lots of manufacturers agree with consumers that goods made in this way are more likely to be of higher quality (consider Toyota's controversial decision to replace robots with more trained craftsmen). This has led to the concept of "artisanal manufacturing," a practice that, if more broadly embraced, could lead to significant decrease in the environmental impact of manufacturing, as well as to an increase of jobs based locally in the U.S.

Manufacturing in America as opposed to manufacturing in China now only represents a 5% difference in cost, a massive decrease from price differences in the past. For those manufacturers continuing their operations overseas, developing financial changes at home and aboard coupled with the added cost of transporting goods to and from overseas locations will likely make the value of investing in reshoring and joining the reshoring movement a practical financial reality.

Chapter 11: The Return of Manufacturing

One way President Obama acquired a reputation for being "hostile to business" was his propensity to pose awkward questions to business leaders. In February 2011, for instance, in the middle of a breakfast with the titans of Silicon Valley, President Obama declined to offer the kind of adulation to which these warrior gods of the C-suite have become accustomed. Instead, he interrupted Steve Jobs, the legendary CEO of Apple, and asked what it would take to make iPhones in the United States.

"Those jobs are gone," Jobs is said to have snapped back, like a professor to a student who hadn't done his homework, "And they're not coming back."

Sadly, Steve Jobs himself is now gone, but it turns out that some of the manufacturing jobs that were systematically shipped overseas for several decades in the process, devastating US manufacturing and the US economy are now coming back to America. Admittedly, the return flow is still a trickle, compared to the flood of industries that have been abandoned to other countries. What took decades to lose can't be rebuilt overnight; but the signs are undeniable. US manufacturing is making something of a comeback.

GE is spending some $800 million, to re-establish manufacturing in its giant facility; until recently, almost defunct at Appliance Park, in Louisville,

Kentucky. In February 2012, GE opened an all-new assembly line to make cutting-edge, low-energy water heaters. In March 2012, GE started a second assembly line to make new high-tech French-door refrigerators. Another assembly line is under construction make a new stainless-steel dishwasher starting in early 2013. "I don't do that because I run a charity," Jeff Immelt, CEO of GE, said at a public event in September. "I do that because I think we can do it here and make more money."

Changes in relative economics are part of the reasons for the change. Oil prices are three times what they were in 2000. Natural gas in the US is a quarter of what it is in Asia. Chinese wages are five times what they were in 2000 and are expected to keep rising rapidly and labour is a steadily decreasing percentage of the cost of manufacturing.

Even more important than these shifts in prices is the growing realization that the massive international outsourcing that took place over the past few decades didn't make sense in the first place.

Just five years ago, not to mention 10 or 20 years ago, the unchallenged logic of the global economy was that you couldn't manufacture much besides a fast-food hamburger in the United States... There was no reason design and marketing could not take place in one country while production, from the start, happened half a world away.

But a funny thing happened, when GE decided to bring manufacturing of its innovative GeoSpring water heater back from the "cheap" Chinese factory to the "expensive" Kentucky factory.

The material cost went down. The labour required to make it went down. The quality went up. Even the energy efficiency went up. GE wasn't just able to hold the retail sticker to the 'China price.' It beat that price by nearly 20 percent. The China-made GeoSpring retailed for $1,599. The Louisville-made GeoSpring retails for $1,299.

Time-to-market also improved, greatly. It used to take five weeks to get the GeoSpring water heaters from the factory to U.S. retailers; four weeks on the boat from China and one week dockside to clear customs. Today, the water heaters and the dishwashers and refrigerators move straight from the manufacturing buildings to Appliance Park's warehouse out back, from which they can be delivered to Lowe's and Home Depot. Total time from factory to warehouse; 30 minutes.

Similarly the Whirlpool water tower is a powerful symbol of the heart of Clyde's economy. Visitors to Clyde are greeted with the view of a water tower presiding over the flat landscape, carrying a large Whirlpool logo. The tower is a clear symbol of the small Ohio town's economic heart.

Whirpool's 2.5 million sq ft (232,000 sq m) washing machine factory dominates the main drag of Clyde and the businesses along this stretch, such as Gary's Diner and Pizza House, are often filled with the appliance manufacturer's workers.

On the factory floor, the noise is overwhelming. More than 3,000 workers; half the population of Clyde are busy testing, screwing, welding, and painting the hundreds of pieces that make up the company's washing machines.

This is the largest washing machine plant in the world, with 30 miles (50km) of overhead conveyor belts that clatter along, carrying assorted barrel drums and metal doors.

Sonny Workman Assembly worker Sonny Workman says Whirlpool is "the family business"

But stop for the time it takes to make one machine - approximately four seconds and a few things will become apparent that differ from factories past.

Those carts driving by, filled with grey fabric? They have no driver. They are automated to follow an orange line on the ground and those LED screens at each assembly line? They monitor each worker's productivity to the second and can give instant feedback about how to improve production.

Such details make the plant one of Whirlpool's most productive, and it is one reason why the company, when it was looking to move production from a plant in Mexico, decided to bring jobs back to Ohio.

"There's been a lot of focus both by the company and the employees to become more efficient, more effective," says Whirlpool vice president Jeff Noel.

"That's made making products in the US more competitive than it has been in the past."

Homecoming

American manufacturing lost more than two million jobs during the recession, accelerating a decline that had begun long ago in the 1970s.

Yet since then, manufacturing has been one of the biggest drivers of job growth in the US, adding more than 500,000 jobs.

While much of that job growth could be attributable to post-recession pent-up demand, that is not the whole story. About 10% of those job gains; 50,000 jobs were created by companies bringing back manufacturing from overseas.

Better, faster, more productive

These days, making washing machines in the US is competitive

There are many reasons why the corporate accounts are once again favouring the American worker.

Higher labour costs abroad, coupled with cheap natural gas as a result of the fracking boom in the US and workers who are willing to work for lower wages, have made it more economical than it once was to produce back in America.

Moreover, changing consumer behaviour means customers often want products immediately and with varying specifications, so it's better to be closer to your customers.

Finally, newer factories with increasingly automated technology require a more highly educated workforce, which the US has as a result of its manufacturing past. Besides, automation costs are roughly the same wherever in the world a company operates.

With all these factors combined, by 2016 a variety of manufacturing industries, from appliances to tyres, will find it more cost effective to produce goods in the United States, according to a recent report.

This could add an estimated two to three million jobs and more than $20bn in output to the American economy; a striking reversal from years past.

Chapter 12: More Companies Reshoring

In 2005, a start-up company from California called ET Water Systems decided to move its manufacturing operations to China. At the time there was a general exodus to Asia in search of lower costs. ET Water Systems, which builds sophisticated irrigation devices for businesses, quickly started losing money, not least because it had so much capital tied up in big shipments of goods which took weeks to cross the oceans. Innovation suffered from the distance between manufacturing and design, and quality became a problem too.

Five years later the company investigated the difference between the total cost of production in China and America, including the cost of shipping, customs duties and other fees, he was amazed to find that California was only about 10% more expensive than China and that was just on the immediate numbers, without allowing for the intangible benefits of making the devices almost next door. ET Water Systems' new manufacturing partner, General Electronics Assembly, is in San Jose. As it happens, the firm's owner has a Chinese background and a large portion of its employees are of South-East Asian origin.

The number of firms known to have "reshored" manufacturing to America is well under 100. Doubtless many more are doing so quietly. Examples range from the tiny, such as ET Water Systems, to the enormous, such as General Electric, which moved manufacturing of washing machines, fridges and heaters back from China to a factory in Kentucky which not long ago had been expected to close. Google has attracted a great deal of attention for deciding to make its Nexus Q, a new media streamer, in San Jose.

The reshoring movement has to be kept in proportion. Most of the multinationals involved are bringing back only some of their production destined for the American market. Much of what they had moved over the past few decades remains overseas and for many of the biggest firms the amount of work that they are still sending abroad outweighs the amount that they are bringing back onshore. Caterpillar, for example, is opening a new factory in Texas to make excavators, but has also just announced that it will expand its research and development activities in China.

We could argue that firms are now ready to reconsider offshoring. They realise that in many cases they overdid it, and are discovering hidden costs in moving production a long way from home; but we argue, America's government is not making the country's business environment attractive enough for companies to want to come back.

Given the political pressure, it is natural for companies to want to publicise anything that looks like reshoring. Lenovo says that its decision to bring back computer-making to North Carolina was a way of looking after the firm's reputation as well as bringing direct business benefits. The Chinese firm's global supply-chain chief, Gerry Smith, says he has received dozens of telephone calls from former university classmates to congratulate him on the move.

Reshoring amounts to much more than public relations. It is being driven by powerful forces and will only get stronger. In a survey of American manufacturing companies by the Boston Consulting Group (BCG) in April 2012, 37% of those with annual sales above $1 billion said they were planning or actively considering shifting production facilities from China to America. Of the very biggest firms, with sales above $10 billion, 48% came out as reshorers. The most common reason given was higher Chinese labour costs. The Massachusetts Institute of Technology looked at 108 American manufacturing firms with multinational operations last summer. It found that 14% of them had firm plans to bring some manufacturing back to America and one-third were actively considering such a move.

A study last year by the Hackett Group, a Florida-based firm that advises companies on offshoring and outsourcing, produced similar results. It expects the outflow of manufacturing from high to low-cost countries to slow over the next two years and the reshoring to double over the previous two years. The offshoring of manufacturing is now rapidly moving towards equilibrium zero net offshoring.

The crucial change that has taken place over the past decade or so is that wages in low-cost countries have soared. According to the International Labour Organisation, real wages in Asia between 2000 and 2008 rose by 7.1-7.8% a year. Pay for senior management in several emerging markets, such as China, Turkey and Brazil, now either matches or exceeds pay in America and Europe, according to a recent study by the Hay Group, a consulting firm. Pay in advanced economies, on the other hand, rose by just 0.5% to 0.9% a year between 2000 and 2008, says the McKinsey Global Institute. In manufacturing, the financial crisis actually reduced pay; real wages in American manufacturing have declined by 2.2% since 2005.

By contrast, pay and benefits for the average Chinese factory worker rose by 10% a year between 2000 and 2005 and speeded up to 19% a year between 2005 and 2010, according to BCG. The Chinese government has set a target for annual increases in the minimum wage of 13% until 2015. Strikes are becoming more frequent, and when they happen, says one executive, the government often tells the plant manager to meet workers' demands immediately. Following labour unrest, wages at some factories have gone up steeply. Honda, a Japanese carmaker, gave its Chinese workers a 47% pay rise after strikes in 2010. Foxconn Technology Group, a subsidiary of Hon Hai Precision Industries, a Taiwanese firm that does a lot of manufacturing for Apple and other big technology firms, doubled pay at its factory complex in Shenzhen after a series of suicides. Its labour troubles are still continuing.

BCG used to argue that companies unwilling to send their manufacturing to lower-cost countries were putting their very future in jeopardy. Now it says that companies will bring manufacturing back to America from China. As soon as 2015, says Hal Sirkin, a consultant at the firm, it will cost about the same to manufacture goods for the American market in certain parts of America as in China in many industries, including computers and electronics, machinery, appliances, electrical equipment and furniture. That calculation takes into account a wide variety of direct costs, including labour, property and transport, as well as indirect ones such as supply-chain risk.

After decades of complaining about American and European workers' high pay, cushy conditions and unreasonable expectations, businesspeople now increasingly moan about Chinese workers. Their aspirations are rising and they are less willing to work long hours in boring factory jobs. A new labour law introduced in 2008 brought in more protection for workers, including the right to a permanent contract after a year of employment, and workers are more aware of their rights. One consultant jokes that it is getting as hard to fire people in China as in France.

"China's labour market is so overstretched that all the high-quality labour has been exhausted, you have to hire people with lesser qualifications, and then quality becomes a problem," says Alain Deurwaerder, who until recently ran a factory in Thailand for Ducati, an Italian motorbike-maker. Another European chief executive complains about the flightiness of his

Chinese workforce; "If someone on the other side of the road offers 5% more pay, they go."

Lorne Schaefer, the owner of Jenlo Apparel Manufacturing, a Canadian-owned clothing company, opened a factory in Liuzhou in southern China in 2008 because he could no longer find workers at home; second-generation Chinese and Vietnamese immigrants in Montreal, he says, no longer want to work in the industry. Now he is having similar problems in China. The latest generation of workers, thin on the ground because of the country's one-child policy, are not keen to toil in factories, nor do they want to work for companies that make goods for export, since the quality standards are far higher than for domestic consumption. So even in a labour-intensive industry such as textiles, the cost benefit that China offers is quickly eroding.

Higher labour costs alone are not enough to prompt companies to leave China. The country has the world's best supply chains of components for industry and its infrastructure works well. Firms have already invested heavily in being there and companies that initially came for the low labour costs now want to stay because it has become a huge market in its own right. Nonetheless, "the incremental decision to invest in new production capacity in China has become tricky," says Gordon Orr, Asia chairman for McKinsey.

One answer is to invest in other low-cost countries, of which there is no shortage. Myanmar, for instance, is attracting interest now that the West is lifting economic sanctions; but the scale, skill and productivity of the labour force there, and in countries such as Vietnam and Cambodia, nowhere near matches China's, argues Mr Sirkin and workers in those countries, too, are demanding better pay and rights.

Mexico, which has the huge advantage of bordering the United States, is increasingly attracting production destined for the Americas that would formerly have gone to China. Average pay for Mexican manufacturing workers is now only slightly higher than for Chinese ones, and the time it takes for goods to travel to North America is measured in days not months. Some firms, such as Chrysler, a car company, are even using Mexico as a base to supply the Chinese market. The country has become an important production hub for the aerospace industry; but Mexico's poor infrastructure and highly publicised drugs-related violence may deter some firms.

Even as pay is rising rapidly in China, costs in America are falling. The successful extraction of natural gas from shale has dramatically lowered the price of energy. PricewaterhouseCoopers, an accountancy firm, reckons that these lower American energy prices could result in one million more manufacturing jobs as firms build new factories. Companies such as Dow Chemical, a speciality chemicals firm, and Vallourec, a French steel-tubes firm, have announced new investments in America to take advantage of low gas prices and to supply extraction equipment.

Not only have American wages declined or are rising only slightly, BCG points out, but the dollar has been weakening. The workforce is becoming more flexible and productivity continues to rise. High unemployment has brought a willingness to work for lower pay, especially in southern states. These are mostly "right to work" states where individuals are free to decide whether to give financial support to a trade union, so unions are less powerful there. The very threat that jobs will be outsourced will also have played a role in keeping wages down.

Alabama, one such state, received a big boost last year when Airbus, a European aeroplane manufacturer, said it would open a big new factory. Airbus also plans to expand its production in Asia beyond its main factory in Tianjin, China, to be close to fast-growing new markets. Fabrice Brégier, the firm's chief executive, says that for skilled workers, "China is no longer a low-cost country."

Big unions in America have sometimes been willing to let wages fall to keep jobs at home. In 2007 the United Auto Workers union (UAW) accepted a two-tier wage structure under which some new blue-collar workers are paid only half as much as longer-serving ones. In 2011, after the government had bailed out part of the motor industry, the Big Three carmakers employed more second-tier workers, reducing their overall labour costs. Ford has brought back production from China and Mexico to Ohio and Michigan, thanks to a new agreement with the UAW.

As the example of ET Water Systems showed, transport costs are playing a big part in reshoring. Rising shipping, rail and road costs are most damaging for companies that make goods with relatively low "value-density", such as consumer goods, appliances and furniture, according to a recent McKinsey report on global manufacturing. That makes reshoring or nearshoring more attractive. Emerson, an electrical-equipment maker, has moved factories from Asia to Mexico and North America to be closer to its customers. IKEA, a Swedish firm that makes products for the home, has opened its first factory in North America as a way to cut delivery costs, and Desa, a power-tools firm, has returned production from China to America because savings on transport and raw materials offset the higher labour costs.

In the longer term reshoring will be boosted by the use of advanced manufacturing techniques that promise to alter the economics of production, making it a far less labour-intensive process. 3-D printing, a process in which individual machines build products by depositing layer upon layer of material, is already being used in research departments and factories. Disney is developing 3-D printed lighting for interactive toys, and says that in future the interactive devices inside such toys may be printed rather than assembled by hand. Additive manufacturing machines can be left alone to print day and night. For now they are used mainly for prototyping and for complex parts, but in future they will increasingly make final products too.

Robots are already making a difference to the share of labour in total costs. Cheaper, more user-friendly and more dextrous robots are currently spreading into factories around the world, and they cost just the same in America as they do in China. Relative to the cost of labour, average robot prices since 1990 have fallen by 40-50% in many advanced economies, according to McKinsey. Baxter, a new generation of robot made by Rethink Robotics, an American firm, costs $22,000 apiece and is so safe and simple that it can be taught by an unskilled worker and operate right next to real people.

Baxter and his ilk may mean there will be fewer manufacturing jobs overall, but those that remain can stay close to a firm's domestic headquarters and even if the manufacturing activity itself does not employ many people, the supply chains that spring up around it will create new work.

Chapter 13: Walmart is Giving Priority to U.S. Manufacturers

Walmart is accelerating its program to purchase billions of dollars of more products from U.S based manufacturers. Walmart recently held its first-ever Made in USA 'Open Call' Event" at its Arkansas headquarters. Five-hundred manufacturers pitched their products to Walmart buyers. The only requirement was that their products be manufactured or assembled in the United States. It was the first time in Walmart's history that the company made its buyers available in an open call.

Anybody who wanted an appointment got an appointment, the only caveat is it had to be made or assembled in the U.S. to create American jobs.

Walmart is not backing off its goal of buying $250 billion in additional items from American producers over the next decade. "We are ahead of where we thought we would be after one year," said Walmart spokesman Kory Lundberg. "We are very excited about how it is going."

Walmart also held its second "Manufacturing Summit" focused on identifying U.S. manufacturers that make component parts (such as small motors) that go into products made and assembled by larger U.S based Walmart suppliers. Walmart realizes that it can act as a catalyst in rejuvenating withered U.S. supply chains. "There are opportunities for us to create manufacturing hubs in this country again like we did many years ago," says CEO Simon.

At the first open-call event, Simon told an assembled crowd of 800 manufacturing company representatives that buying a lot more U.S made goods was essential for putting the United States back on stable economic footing. He encouraged other retailers to take up the charge, quickly, in order to improve the economic outlook for the U.S. retail sector.

Walmart has a lot at stake. Without customers, Walmart cannot grow and without manufacturing, Walmart does not have enough customers. The service economy is not generating enough wealth, say Walmart executives. Movie theatres and restaurants cannot sustain a local economy when everyone has a job working at movie theatres and restaurants and can't afford to see movies or eat at restaurants.

When Walmart buys products made by American manufacturing workers, "we see growth in local consumer markets that we haven't seen growth in many, many years," said Simon. "After six years of moving sideways and waiting for something to happen, it is time for American businesses to lead the renewal and growth cycle that will restore the manufacturing base and help grow our economy. We have to do it. We have to do it. We can't wait for government programs and policies that will come and go and will be favourable and unfavourable. We can't wait any more."

Walmart is seeing economic rejuvenation in the communities in which production for Walmart stores is being re-established. Winnsboro, S.C., is experiencing a revival thanks to a new Element Electronics factory that assembles televisions for Walmart that were previously made in China. In Clarendon, S.C., Kent Bicycles is ramping up production to assemble half a million recreational bicycles for Walmart, the first time in a generation that a volume bicycle production facility has been operational in the United States. "They are in discussions with suppliers of component parts for those bicycles to grow around their facility in South Carolina," says Simon. "That is jobs for communities that need those jobs."

In addressing the U.S. manufacturing reps at Walmart headquarter, Simon said that he told the company's buyers to be flexible; to work with companies to help them become Walmart suppliers. "We will have a bias toward 'yes,' " he said. "We want to get to 'yes.' Don't make your decision on what is, but what could be and we will work with you on the 'what could be' part," he told the American manufacturers.

Duncan Mac Naughton, Walmart's Chief Merchandising and Marketing Officer, told the manufacturing reps that Walmart buyers do not want to hear them say, "We can't do it." He offered this advice to the manufacturing companies. "Don't say no. Say, collaboratively, how can we find a path to win together."

Walmart's executives are getting inspiration from founder Sam Walton. "His vision is still what we aspire to deliver," said Simon. "He was bold, he took risks and he moved fast. Let's get some deals done and start to change America."

Michelle Gloeckler, Walmart Executive Vice President of Consumables and U.S. Manufacturing, told the assembled American manufacturers that Walmart will work with any manufacturer on ramping up U.S. production of competitive products. "We talked to our buyers and told them to understand your production output," she said. Smaller manufacturing companies that win supply contracts can phase up production. "We can look at launching them at two distribution centres or launching them on Walmart.com."

Chief Merchandising and Marketing Officer Mac Naughton was more specific; "We are looking at our business one store at a time."

When Walmart contracted with 1888 Mills to make towels in the United States, the company did not have the production capacity to supply 4,000 stores. The manufacturer started by supplying 200 stores, added another 200 and then another 200 as it ramped up production. "As they build their capacity we will continue to make shelf space available to them in more stores," says Walmart spokesman Lundberg.

Sales of towels made by 1888 Mills have increased by 24 percent compared to the towels they replaced that were made in China. Producing those towels in the

United States has reduced Walmart's inventory and has allowed it to order on demand.

1888 Mills is not yet up to 4,000 stores. "They are working on it and they have purchased a new factory in Georgia that they are retrofitting and bringing back to life so they will be able to produce more," says Lundberg.

Other companies have started out in 50 Walmart stores. "We want to figure out what works for you and what works for us and start the process," says Lundberg.

In order to provide companies the ability to ramp up or reshore production, Walmart is providing them with multi-year agreements "with a lot of transparency with the supplier to give people the certainty they need to invest capital in the U.S. to create jobs," said Gloeckler.

Walmart hopes that other retailers start similar "Buy American" programs. "If other retailers get involved and join us, it increases what we are able to do," says Lundberg. "We think we can source $250 billion additional by ourselves, but if the retail industry comes along, just think of what that means?"

Walmart CEO Simon feels the company's Buy American initiative is a transformative event in American history. When he met with all of the company's buyers about the open call, "I said, 'Each and every day our buyers make decisions that impact the lives of our customers; and each and every day, they make decisions that impact their careers and our company.'" But when buyers meet companies interested in producing products in the United States, it "will impact not only our mutual customers and our companies but our country," said Simon. "I believe that today, we are on the edge of a truly great breakthrough and nothing less than the future of the country is at stake. We can do it. I know we can. If we do this right, people will look back and say we really did what our customers needed us to do; that we really, really did what was right for our companies and that we really helped grow the economy of the United States of America."

Of the 500 manufacturers that made a pitch to Walmart on July 8, 56 percent of them were companies that had never sold anything to Walmart. Other Walmart current suppliers pitched new products that could be manufactured in the United States.

"One of the reasons for the open call event was to see what is out there that we don't know about that we should be carrying," says Lundberg. "We saw a lot of great items and made a lot of deals on the spot and we are working with others that are under consideration. It was an amazing event for the suppliers that were here and we will have new products on Walmart.com and in Walmart stores as a result of that." American-made products are being promoted separately on Walmart's consumer web site.

Walmart has found that there are five categories of products that lend themselves to being made in the United States.

1. Products for which raw materials are available at competitive prices, such as cotton, plastics and metals.
2. Products that are made on highly automated production lines that require little manual labour.
3. Products that are slow and inefficient to ship that are bulky, light and take up a lot of space and where freight is a big portion of the price getting the product to the United States.
4. Products where energy is a big part of the production process since energy costs are much lower and power is more reliable in the United States.
5. Products for which there is growing demand; seasonal products or trendy products that need to be quickly restocked.

"Changes in energy and transportation costs and all the variables that make up manufacturing components are swinging in the direction of the United States for the first time in a generation or more and it makes sense to make products closer to our customers; it is more efficient to do that," said Simon.

The Walmart executives describing the Buy American initiative were consistent in describing the number-one attribute Walmart is looking for in a U.S. producer; competitive pricing. "Let's be clear about what our customers expects. It about the right price," said Charles Redfield, Chief Merchandising Officer of Walmart's Sam's Club division. Mac Naughton was more specific: "We have to win and we will win on price." He said Walmart buyers are "respectfully real" with U.S. manufacturers. "If your offer is not competitive, we will tell you. We will coach you. We will work together to make it more competitive."

The company has created a website and email (madeinus@walmart.com) that allows U.S. manufacturers to contact Walmart buyers to pitch U.S made products that Walmart can carry. Companies can find out what it takes to set up an appointment with a Walmart buyer. It has also issued a broad request for proposals seeking U.S. manufacturers of patio furniture. There is also information on future U.S. Manufacturing Summit, to which it invites Walmart suppliers, mass, discount and specialty retailers, raw materials and component suppliers, representatives from state and federal government and financial institutions and investors. For more details visit. http://news.walmart.com/events/2014-us-manufacturing-summit

I encourage Retail giants in the UK to replicate this initiative in the UK and I call on Walmart to lead the initiative through Asda stores in the UK.

Chapter 14: Reshoring Brings Back Multiple Strategic Benefits for Companies

The reshoring logic applies to all manufacturing companies in their sourcing decisions. As companies adopt a more comprehensive total cost analysis, they are finding that rising offshore labour rates (going up by 18 percent per year in China, and 500 percent in the last 12 years), when added to the "hidden costs" of offshoring, often have closed the cost advantage. Common "hidden costs" include travel, carrying cost of inventory, emergency air freight, and the impact on innovation from separating engineering from manufacturing.

Another hidden cost is millions of counterfeit and scrap electronic components (predominantly from China) getting into U.S. military and other systems. The U.S. government has produced numerous reports on the dangers of counterfeit components to national defence. Users of high-precision products such as the military and aerospace and medical equipment companies simply cannot afford the risks of using under-regulated manufacturers found oversees. They are therefore shifting production back to the U.S., where quality and compliance standards remain the highest in the world and where it can be more easily monitored. While the quality standards associated with "Made in USA" or in other developed countries are sometimes essential for high-precision products,

"Made in USA" branding offers value across all sectors of manufacturing.

Zentech, a Maryland company that manufactures electronic systems for a wide range of customers, including defence contractors, medical diagnostics makers, and telecommunications firms, reshored over $1 million in manufacturing in 2012, with plans to reshore even more in 2014. President and CEO Matt Turpin reports the company "is experiencing growth in all industry sectors and continues to see opportunities in the area of reshoring."

Turpin continues; "CEOs and CFOs are realizing that total cost of ownership (TCO) for off-shore manufactured goods is rising even faster than per-unit costs for the same items. Since focusing on reshoring, Zentech experienced a 50 percent growth in its customer base in 2012, and is forecast to increase revenues by as much in 2013. Many of these new customers have the ability to utilize offshore EMS (electronic manufacturing services) providers but fortunately understand the TCO implications."

Zentech's customers cite reasons in their decision to reshore that are common complaints; inventory carrying costs, supply disruption, intellectual property risk, and the need for compliance. Companies that reshore routinely achieve inventory reductions of 50 percent. Some published cases mention reducing inventory by factors of three or even six. The reasons behind inventory reduction include better payment terms, smaller stocking quantities, shorter lead times, and more certainty delivery dates and quality.

Reshoring at least a portion of what has been offshored is a beneficial strategic decision for many companies. But the benefits extend beyond individual companies. The reshoring trend in the U.S. adds jobs, reduces the severity of recessions, helps balance the trade deficit, helps balance budget deficits at all levels, and makes recruiting the next generation of the skilled workforce easier.

Recent reshoring decisions by Apple, Caterpillar, GE, and others suggest that millions of jobs could be reshored in the next 10 years.

Chapter 15: Reshoring is the Latest Phenomenon

Forget the era of "Made in China". The latest business phenomenon is "reshoring", where companies in America and Britain are bringing manufacturing home.

In the UK, the weakness of sterling has made the prospect of repatriating jobs even more alluring. Food manufacturer Symington's is reported to be moving its noodle-making operation from Guangzhou, China, back to Leeds, Yorkshire. The company, which also makes pasta sauce Ragu and Chicken Tonight, is creating 50 jobs in the process.

Henrik Pade, business development manager at Symington's, said "it now costs roughly the same to make Golden Wonder pot noodles in Yorkshire as it does China.

"Everybody prefers to do manufacturing on their own doorstep rather than far away, which means you need to have a financial incentive to outsource", he said. The firm said it had once cost 30-35 per cent less to make the noodles in China, but wage inflation there and freight costs had pushed up production costs.

Symington's is just the latest company to try reshoring. The clothing manufacturers Top Shop and

River Island have also been purchasing more materials from domestic suppliers.

We can safely claim "offshoring" is now "yesterday's model". 40 per cent of manufacturers have brought some of their capacity back to the UK, up from one in seven companies in 2009.

The phenomenon isn't confined to the UK. As stated earlier in this book US manufacturing giant General Electric has repatriated jobs from China to its vast plant in Louisville, Kentucky.

The changes are part of a "global rebalancing" of economies as Asia grows richer. US President Barack Obama highlighted the trend in his State of the Union address, saying: "After shedding jobs for more than 10 years, our manufacturers have added about 500,000 jobs over the past three".

While the repatriation of these jobs sounds positive, there is a downside; they tend to be poorly paid. The jobs that are coming back are typically lower pay, sometimes lower benefits, than the jobs that were lost.

Chapter 16: Is UK Ready for the Return of Manufacturing?

We are hearing a lot about onshoring from the industry and with increases in transport costs, rising wages in China and a more competitive exchange rate, the prognosis is good for the return of manufacturing to the UK, but I must ask the question whether we have sufficient skilled labour to take advantage of this opportunity.

Despite unemployment levels of around eight per cent (2.5 million people) in the first half of 2012, apprenticeship places remain unfilled and the level of skilled workers in many manufacturing facilities is still well below that required. While manufacturing production in the UK fell in May 2012 by 1.7 per cent over last year according to the Office of National Statistics, there are strong indicators that this tide will turn with companies returning to, or expanding production in, the UK; however, we believe that the skills shortage could seriously disrupt any potential growth in the sector and growth will only be achieved if companies have the right people in the right jobs.

Toyota chooses to manufacture engines at its plant in Burnaston, Deeside, UK and ship them back to Japan.

The drive to move business back to the UK is not just about labour costs. Companies such as BT and Santander returned their call centres to the UK because the customers demanded it. In manufacturing circles, Toyota produces the new hybrid engine at the UK plant in Deeside and then ships this back to Japan for installation, reminding us that production should not only be where it is most cost-effective but also where you can guarantee the standard of production and delivery required by customers.

The increasing cost of raw materials, transportation and the complexity of supply chains are also major considerations when considering plant location. It has taken harsh lessons in reality for companies to realise the fully loaded cost, not just the unit cost, has to be measured. Aside from the increasing costs already mentioned, there have always been 'hidden' costs associated with offshoring that, when considered, paint a slightly different picture. For instance, it is almost always necessary to engage a local agent to act as an interface with the supplier. There are long lead times, minimum-order quantities that necessitate holding more stock, this impacts upon cash flow and increases the danger of stock obsolescence. There is additional travel costs, as well as the difficulties arising from language and time-zone differences.

We have seen the effect of onshoring already in the US with companies such as Caterpillar opting to relocate its new plants in the US. The driving force for this was increased shipping costs, supply-chain complexity and inconsistent quality, which meant that the offshore plants were just not competitive.

The increasing cost of raw materials, transportation and the complexity of supply chains are also major considerations when considering plant location.

Manufacturing is quite rightly back in the spotlight, but it needs a concerted investment in training, and a 'make-over' to ensure that it attracts the right candidates, so that it can once again serve as the catalyst for prosperity. The sector spurs demand for everything from raw materials and intermediate components to software and services of all kinds. Studies and statistics show that manufacturing significantly impacts upon the widespread creation of jobs-and wealth.

So why is manufacturing facing such a remarkable problem? Unfortunately, the old stereotypes of back-breaking labour and grimy working conditions persist. Ask people today what they think of manufacturing and most will probably describe dirty, dangerous work that requires little thinking or skill, and offers minimal opportunity for personal growth or career advancement. This is totally inaccurate.

Today's manufacturing jobs are 'cool' and appealing. Workers are now required to be experts and operate the most sophisticated equipment in the world. They can cut steel with lasers, water jets and plasma cutters and can program robots to paint, package and palletise products. Computer programming and other high-tech skills are needed, which dovetails precisely with what younger people love these days; these jobs can be more fun and, ultimately, more satisfying than many service-sector jobs.

To be fair, the government has made some steps to address this but much more needs to be done to ensure we capitalise on the opportunity presented and ensure the multinationals see the UK as the most viable option for their manufacturing plants.

Chapter 17: Reshoring is on the Rise in United Kingdom

The ebb and flow of global economic tides is increasingly turning in favour of the UK with a growing number of manufacturing businesses bringing back work to British shores.

A major new report released recently found that one in six companies has "reshored" production in the past three years, up from one in seven when a similar study was carried out in 2009.

Having once looked to cut costs by moving production to low-cost emerging nations, more and more businesses are heeding Prime Minister David Cameron's call in his World Economic Forum speech to come home as these countries' economies mature and labour costs rise, according to the report Backing Britain; a manufacturing base for the future; but cost isn't the only reason. Other factors include capitalising on Britain's reputation for excellence, the ability to create shorter, more responsive supply chains and ease of communication with customers.

The trend may be gradual but it is highly encouraging to see more reshoring. While it will always be two-way traffic, the need to be closer to customers, to have ever greater control of quality and the continued erosion of low labour costs in some competitor countries mean that in many cases it makes increasingly sound business sense.

The UK's manufacturing sector has undergone huge changes over the past few decades, with the relatively high domestic cost base meaning it has stopped focusing on price and now concentrates on offering quality and expertise.

This means manufacturers have to deliver every time; something that can be a problem with factories on the other side of the world and long supply chains.

With speed to market becoming ever more important and manufacturers seeking greater flexibility to respond to customer requirements, the value of shorter supply chains is on the increase. Among the top reasons for reshoring is greater certainty around shorter delivery times.

About a third of companies said this was the prime reason to reshore.

Meeting deadlines is also of extreme importance, with almost a quarter saying the reliability that comes with domestic production was the reason for bringing it home. This challenge has been heightened by a number of recent events and disruptions from natural disasters and recession to international transport failures and increasingly congested cargo terminals.

Fluctuating transport costs were also cited by some respondents as a factor.

Meeting the standards required to deliver high-quality products was the prime reason for reshoring production for many companies, but particularly so for smaller businesses where reputation is all and losing a contract because a product did not come up to specification could see a company fail. Quality was the prime reason in 50% of the cases of reshoring among smaller companies.

Almost half of manufacturers believe the quality of goods sourced from lower labour cost countries is getting better, with larger companies seemingly better able to secure quality improvements, but confidence that overseas operators will supply to the required specification is not sufficient to many.

The benefits of moving work closer to home are also being felt on a pure financial basis for many. Although 3% of the companies said their revenue fell as a result of reshoring, half said it remained stable and two fifths saw it rise. Interestingly, more report seeing profits increase rather than turnover, with three in five saying profits had risen as a result of reshoring.

Inevitably, reshoring delivers a jobs boost but the increase is small, the report found. More than two thirds said employee numbers either remained stable or rose by between 1% and 5%, however, the jobs brought home tend to be worth having, with the report noting that they "are likely to be highly skilled, technical and well paid".

Reshoring is not without its problems; common issues cited were disruption to production, taking up management time and finding suppliers.

In line with the Coalition's drive to rebalance the British economy, We are now calling on policymakers to take on board the report's findings. We wants ministers to "think long term. Developing new products, fostering new suppliers and investing in new capacity delivers returns measured in years for many businesses. Government decision-making in many key areas such as tax, skills, climate change policy and our relationship with Europe must become more aligned with the reality of manufacturing investment cycles.

It is now key that government policy supports the most competitive business environment possible so that we continue to see more companies backing Britain and bringing production back to the UK.

Chapter 18: Made in Britain

"EEF" is the largest sectoral employers' organisation in the UK. It aims to build an environment in which manufacturing businesses can evolve, innovate and compete in a fast-changing world.

Luxury chocolate brand Hotel Chocolat chose to reshore in order to protect their vision as well as to keep ideas in-house

The Far East has become the centre of manufacturing thanks to cheap labour. But as costs rise with a burgeoning middle-class in the east and rising shipping costs, many brands are bringing manufacturing back to the UK.

The return of manufacturing from offshore to the UK and other developed economies is more than just a rumour.

The findings confirmed those from a 2009 survey, when one in seven had reshored, and they have been heralded by many as signs of a rebirth in British manufacturing. Indeed, in a further poll of EEF members at the organisation's 2014 conference, they were almost unanimous in declaring that reshoring would help drive UK economic growth over the next five years, with 29 per cent saying it would do so significantly.

Reshoring trend could create around 100,000 to 200,000 UK jobs over the next decade and boost annual national output by around £6bn to £12bn at current values by the mid-2020s; that represents a GDP boost of between 0.4 and 0.8 per cent.

Manufacturing could benefit significantly from this trend, with additional UK jobs being created in sectors ranging from textiles to electrical equipment and other machinery.

In the latest EEF survey, the main reason for reshoring to the UK was improving the quality of products and components, closely followed by issues surrounding customer service, speed of delivery and the desire to minimise logistics costs. EEF members also mentioned labour costs and the more general aim of getting closer to customers.

They seem to be seeing results, with 40 per cent of companies saying their turnover had increased as a direct result of reshoring, while only 3 per cent had seen a fall. In addition, 60 per cent of companies said they had seen profits and employment increase, albeit only moderately.

Other voices are more cautious and, of course, the EEF survey implies that a significant proportion of British manufacturers still do production offshore. The other five in six have previously offshored and their objectives are being met.

The reasons for offshoring have changed though; it may have been to gain market access or for regulatory reasons, and the best way to do that was to be there, or it may simply have been to connect with customers there.

What that means is that to manufacture outside the UK is no longer necessarily offshoring. As GKN's CEO Nigel Stein points out, you may be British-headquartered, but if you sell globally you may well need to manufacture globally. "We never offshored," he says. "We follow our customers around the world."

So who is reshoring, who could or should do it and why, who will benefit and were companies wrong to offshore in the first place? The reshoring reasons haven't changed significantly. We see people bringing production back on the basis of quality, supply chain weaknesses and so on.

"When China joined the WTO "World Trade Organization" we couldn't compete, because they could sell cheaper than we could manufacture, so we set up a joint venture there," says Tony Caldeira, CEO of home furnishings company Caldeira. "In the last few years though, Chinese costs have risen significantly faster than in the west and the UK has become more competitive. UK manufacturing has become leaner. We also found the classic reasons of culture, lead times, payment terms; lots of people have had these problems. You need to plan much further ahead when manufacturing in the Far East too, which ties up a lot of working capital and inventory.

Lower labour costs were a big part of why many companies offshored production, but while pay rates in the manufacturing industry in developed countries have stagnated or fallen in the years since the financial bust, in many emerging markets they have climbed dramatically. Pay and benefits for the average Chinese factory worker, for example, rose by 10 per cent a year between 2000 and 2005 and by up to 19 per cent a year between 2005 and 2010.

Transportation costs have risen too and, although they have since settled somewhat they remain volatile, meaning that anyone who offshored on the assumption of cheap shipping has had to re-think. In addition, as the demand for more customised and individual products has risen, it has become less and less attractive to have goods in transit for weeks on end.

Of course high labour and shipping costs on their own will not push all the outsourcers to leave China. The country has a highly developed supply chain for industrial components and a good infrastructure. In addition the local market has grown, so that many of the manufacturers who moved there for cheaper labour are now staying in order to service the Chinese market. For them, what has changed is the decision on where to add extra manufacturing capacity and which elements of the process to do where.

Others are pursuing cheap labour though, moving from China perhaps to Vietnam, Bangladesh or Cambodia, or now that Western economic sanctions are lifting, to Myanmar (Burma). UK CEOs who have already reshored are sceptical.

Most global companies already have a good solution for their low-cost products. In an industry that is very labour intensive maybe you chase cheap production, but because we are more efficient in the UK now, we don't have to chase for the next low-cost labour zone. Chasing labour cost is chasing rainbows.

Angus Thirlwell, the CEO of UK confectionery manufacturer Hotel Chocolat, points out that it is possible that such investment may even become unwelcome to the host nations. "If your business model depends on low-cost, low-skill labour you are going to be chasing developing nations around the world," he says. "But what is that bringing to a developing nation? There is no skill transfer or anything."

It depends on the nature of your business. There can still be some advantage if you have a commodity product, a homogeneous low-cost product where you can give clear instructions.

Labour cost squeeze has even affected China itself; I was struck when I went to China last year, I went to buy some shoes and all the shoes in the shop were made in Vietnam!

But when you are trying to tailor a product more; it's interesting that this came up when we spoke to people in textile manufacturing or where there is fashion involved, a less homogeneous product and people want to order online, you want things close to hand.

Getting the sums wrong

I was once asked; "Still, if offshoring companies failed to spot that there was a lot more to the cost of production than just the factory gate cost, or that the laws of supply and demand would push up Chinese labour costs; if everyone moved their production to China, or that the long-undervalued Chinese currency would eventually be allowed to appreciate, does that make them negligent or short-sighted?"

People had missed subtle things, like the costs of constantly having to send your purchasing people to the other side of the world, the quality of the output and the pressure to maintain decent working conditions, which means you spend more to avoid damage to your reputation.

There is volatility risks from these markets too; exchange rate volatility from capital flows in and out, extreme weather events too. Those may not have been fully factored in. Another reason for reshoring is to make your supply chain more resilient.

Raspberry Pi co-founder Eben Upton agrees; "When you do the sums, it is bill-of-materials and labour for the factory gate cost, but then you have to add shipping, warranty, brand equity," he says. "You have to make an allowance for possible brand damage; you shouldn't weight that at zero, just in case your subcontractor is employing children or has staff jumping off the roof. It is the intangibles and how you price risk.

Is it possible to anticipate those problems?

Every investment carries risks, some of which you can account for, but there is always the unknown unknowns. Our survey did suggest that more companies are considering reshoring, so the trend will continue.

One other factor driving the reshoring trend is the need to be more agile; to shorten supply lines, get closer to UK customers, cut the lead time on expanded orders from four weeks to one, reduce the time needed to introduce new products and so on. A key enabler there is new manufacturing technologies, and of course robots and other new machinery, cost pretty much the same wherever in the world you install them.

We will use digital printing for textiles as an example; this is a fashion business and it means faster delivery and makes lower print runs cost-effective, even in cushion making, technology can bring advantage if it lets you set lower minimum order volumes and respond faster, so we could be setting up a whole new UK production line if digital printing comes off.

Jobless resurgence

But one thing that advanced manufacturing technology doesn't do much for is headcount. The irony of it is it's sort of a jobless resurgence. Of course Sony added more people to make the Raspberry Pi in Wales, but nowhere near as many as they did have needed in the 1980s.

That is particularly true for low-skilled factory work. Companies that have reshored production to the UK or are sourcing more intermediate goods locally have seen a modest increase in headcount, but the nature of those jobs will be different. We are looking at more highly skilled and highly paid jobs now.

That in turn points to one of the main challenges to the reshoring trend, which is the availability of manufacturing skills. Everywhere I go, other than China and India, people say 'It's terrible, we can't get the engineers', and so on.

The skills shortage is a long-term issue across many developed economies; we haven't filled the pipeline with enough people with appropriate STEM skills. We have definitely seen a trend towards more training and in particular the recruitment of apprentices. There has been a lot of change, creating uncertainty over training programmes, but companies are recognising the need now to be responsible for training.

Despite all this, one of the most interesting things that came out of talking to companies that had reshored was that while they had had to train people, the skilled nature of these new jobs aided both recruitment and retention. Once potential recruits realised that this wasn't a dull assembly line job, the choice between being a shelf-stacker and helping to make something was an easy one.

Home furnishings company Caldeira moved production to China in search of lower manufacturing costs, but as Chinese costs rose it discovered that it needed a more nuanced approach. It reshored a big chunk of production to the UK, yet kept some in China, both for materials and to serve local markets.

It means less complications in the supply chain and less shipping, and a lot of the company's customers are now labelling their products as 'Proudly made in the UK.

The company also do a lot of business in the US, and the fact that they are making the product in the UK and not in China carries a lot of weight with some of the company's customers in the U.S.

When they first opened in China in 2003, they thought it would be one-way and nothing would come back. That tide has turned now, and as long as the exchange rate moves in their favour more companies will bring work back. They have always maintained a manufacturing base in the UK; there is a lot of skill and expertise in the UK. They have been fortunate to hold onto that skill-base to an extent; some industries lost it completely when they moved everything.

There are several reasons for keeping some Chinese manufacturing, not least that some British retailers insist on buying FOB Shenzen; they have invested in China themselves, and prefer to buy there. But in many cases it is proximity to market, for example it is not cost-effective to bring manufacture back if the final destination is Australia. Some companies also sell products to Chinese retailers now, which is ironic. There is a lot of aspiration in China for western style.

UK import duties are higher on finished products than on materials, plus there is freight costs, and for example the labour cost in expensive cushions is relatively low. So that enables you to bring that work home, and also get the advantages of lead-time and culture and so on. Some companies will get the best of both worlds by still having China for the base fabric and lower-end products.

Reshoring - Hotel Chocolat

When the founders of over 10-year-old boutique chocolatier Hotel Chocolat looked for manufacturing capacity in an industry whose British heyday was probably the 1920s, the route seemed obvious; outsource to medium-sized family companies in the famous chocolate-producing countries of mainland Europe; however, once they looked closer they realised that their contractors had rather less value to add than anticipated, plus they were concerned about being copied, and within a couple of years they made the decision to reshore.

CEO and co-founder Angus Thirlwell sees that decision as part of a journey of discovery. "We decided to do it ourselves for two reasons; first, all the ideas were coming from us, and the chocolate industry there is very conservative, and second, we wanted to protect our brand and vision," he explains. "We only go out now for things that need special equipment, such as Turkish Delight; the best place for that is Istanbul, so we work with a true specialist there."

Hotel Chocolat built up its Cambridgeshire factory over eight years, and is now vertically integrated from a cocoa plantation in St Lucia to retail stores; a rare thing in this business. "Of course we don't aim to produce all our cocoa," says Thirlwell, adding that you need diverse suppliers partly because different geographies produce different flavours, but also to protect against weather risks and so on.

He continues; "Depending on your business model, reshoring can make a lot of sense; we know now that we can make better, more efficiently and with more agility than our friends in Europe. The old-school way was to set up a factory for a single type of chocolate and there is no way to change it, and that was okay when customers were less demanding. Our factory is set up to be agile, marrying the best of human skills with automation.

What de-risked it for us was we knew we had demand for our product range, so it wasn't a case of building manufacturing capacity in the hope that the product would sell. Offshoring for short-term gains is unsustainable, but outsourcing is fabulous in terms of dipping a toe into the water, into new markets as a start-up, then you bring it back and it scales up."

He adds that the company could well produce abroad again, but to service local markets. "We are hoping to grow in Asia and would certainly consider doing some manufacturing closer to there," he says. "We could make the simpler, faster moving lines out there, and once we achieved scale send out the higher margin products; but then it's local sourcing, not offshoring."

British manufacturing – Raspberry Pi

"We originally went to China because it's a challenge making low volume, low margin stuff in the UK; our first run was 2,000 units," says Eben Upton, CEO of Raspberry Pi (Trading). "Low volume, high margin we are good at; take Formula 1 cars. But the labour costs dominate before you automate, and in China companies have low labour costs, they are close to the component suppliers, and they are keen for business."

He adds: "China is both cheap and not that hard to do business in. The rules in Shenzen are pretty straightforward; a lot of the other places you could build in don't have that." Yet in September 2012, Raspberry Pi announced that it; or strictly speaking its technology licensees would reshore the bulk of production, bringing it to a Sony factory in Wales.

"We didn't bring it back for patriotic reasons, we did it for cost," Upton says, adding that "There is a global goodwill towards British manufacturing; that is the closest I get to saying we are doing it for patriotic reasons.

"What happened was we discovered that as volume grew we could save money by bringing it back. A shorter supply chain is part of that, plus it is not as cheap to ship products from China as it used to be;

the advantage when we moved was within the margin of the shipping cost.

"Plus, larger volumes meant we could automate. What you are left with then is tangible benefits; it's cheaper to build in Wales. You also get the intangible benefits of having your factory at the end of the M4, not a 15-hour flight away, and it speaks the same language too.

"We continue to have a great relationship with our Far Eastern contract manufacturer. We weren't driven back by a horrible experience; those guys are honest and capable, and they built over a million Raspberry Pis. They still have the licence to build Pis for the Far Eastern region, plus on one or two occasions we have needed surge production capacity, and ironically they can be more responsive to that because they are closer to the component suppliers."

Chapter 19: Bringing it All Back Home

A recent survey of 500 small and medium sized manufacturers in the UK has revealed a growing number of companies are bringing production home in order to reduce costs. Some 26% of companies surveyed said that concerns about the cost of offshore production has led to them "reshoring". A desire to improve the quality of products was the second reason, cited by 20% of respondees, followed by 18% who said the move also meant they could reduce lead times.

There is a growing desire to take production home, with 15% of firms reporting that they have or are in the process of bring production back. This is compared to just 4% that have offshored in the last year. This marks a major change in approach from five years ago, when the Far East and Eastern Europe seemed to be the destinations of choice for British companies. Buyers have realised that there is more to the landing price than meets the eye, with delays in logistics and issues around quality adding a layer of costs.

The survey also showed that 68% of firms that have reshored in the last 12 months have reported an increase in sales. Overall, 56% of the firms surveyed said they had increased sales in the last six months; however, the cost of domestic labour remains the biggest barrier to producing within the UK to manufacturing Small and medium enterprises (SMEs) and nearly one in ten are concerned about the availability of the right skills.

There had been a slight reduction in the number of companies looking to recruit. This could reflect that many firms chose to retain skills during the recession and still feel they have enough capacity to cope with their anticipated expansion.

RDM Group, a Coventry-based automotive component supplier, has started manufacturing at a new £400,000 factory in the city of Coventry UK, allowing it to repatriate subcontracted production from China. It will make aluminium rechargeable torches for Jaguar Land Rover at the plant and plans to bring the rest of its China-based work, mostly of moulded products, back by the middle of next year.

RDM has made some components in China for the past eight years. "We went there because it was going to be cheap, but cheap has turned into ever-increasing prices because wages and other costs are rising rapidly," said David Keene, chairman.

Another factor was the need to respond rapidly to customers' needs. "The automotive companies are getting faster and faster in their cycle of delivering products. There is also a lot of personalisation going on," said Mr Keene. "If you have got a supply chain that takes months to bring stuff in, you can't be flexible."

Chapter 20: Technology Manufacturing is Coming Home

Google's Motorola, Apple and Lenovo are manufacturing more and more in the US. It's easy for us to see why firms are shifting work back from the Far East.

Breffo, currently one of the UK's largest manufacturers of consumer electronic accessories, has been manufacturing all its products at its factory in Devon UK, for a number of years now. They have had the fortune of realising the advantages of UK manufacturing from the start and there is most certainly a shift taking place for more companies to reassess the perceived benefits of Far East manufacturing. We have found the shift is based more on strategy over financials.

More recently, manufacturing has moved into a highly technical and highly automated environment. This reduces the need for manual labour, which in turn reduces cost. These associated costs are still cheaper in China than they are in the UK or the US, but as many companies such as Apple and Google and Breffo manufacture with high automation, then the costs to produce become far more even between countries.

Add high quality materials, a highly skilled and educated workforce, low shipping cost and timings and fast efficient turnaround into the mix and manufacturing in the UK or the US becomes a no-brainer.

Companies love being within a few hours drive of many of their customers and suppliers. It allows for a much closer relationship and understanding with the whole market within which they work, which is very important in today's economy. It also allows for much quicker reaction times if needed.

They do not have to deal with long shipping times and their retailers and distributors both here in the UK and across our international markets love the fact that they can turnaround a product and get it shipped within days and not months. This has been a big positive for them and a large competitive advantage.

There are also no language barriers, which can quite often delay a product release or cause issues due to drops in communication or language misinterpretations.

Breffo are at a pivotal point in the new revolution and the company would very much like to be a part of bringing manufacturing back home to the UK.

A rise in labour and energy costs in China's economy has made manufacturing in China significantly more expensive and is driving business out of China and back to places like the US, UK and beyond. Transportation costs have risen too and it is often no longer greatly advantageous to manufacture abroad, especially if this is predominantly automated.

Companies are also tired of the constant legal battles due to the poorly regulated intellectual property market in China. With every new idea shipped to China for production is a real and validated fear of your idea being stolen, copied and produced, even before you get to market. This is not the case in most regions outside China where IP is very well regulated and policed. It is almost a pleasure not having to worry whether the factory that is handling your products is ripping you off out the back door!

We have heard some nightmare stories where copycat products are outselling genuine product all sold from the master manufacturers factory in China. Manufacturing in the UK or US, we don't have to deal with this issue.

So we see this shift as a really positive step for manufacturing in general and for the global market. Higher quality products will certainly be more abundant and although Google are just experimenting with the production of Google Glass in the USA right now, all eyes from the manufacturing and tech world will be on them to see how successful they can be making their products in the US.

Chapter 21: Manufacturing Came Back to Northern Ireland

Nine years ago, Elite Electronic Systems decided to source cables from abroad that it had previously made at its base in Enniskillen, Northern Ireland United Kingdom.

While the plan started well, it soon ran into problems. "Then the recession hit, highlighting the pitfalls of long supply chains," says director Jonathan Balfour.

"Quality was an issue and then we had a recession," he said. "Our Chinese supplier had just received an order which would normally take more than three months to ship. We tried to stop it but; miraculously it was on a ship within two weeks."

Unable to halt the consignment, Elite ended up sitting on 20 months of stock, instead of the normal month or two, hitting the company's cash flow just as the financial crisis was at its worst.

Elite, whose customers include Caterpillar, Chubb and Tyco, also says the sheer physical distance of having production on the other side of the world causes difficulties. "We seemed to have to go out there every time there was a problem, if we wanted to make a change or prototype," Mr Balfour said, adding that travel costs soon racked up.

"Also, it's very difficult to figure out what a customer wants in 20 weeks' time the normal delivery period and a product arriving a week or two late could leave us sitting on months of stock."

Logistics simply exacerbated Elite's troubles, he added. "You have got to find a ship, get the product on to it, get it through customs; we could have consignments sitting in a port for weeks... It was tiring."

Having invested in more efficient equipment at its Enniskillen base, the decision was made to reshore and the company now employs 185 staff in Northern Ireland.

"Elite found itself swept along with the widespread desire to cut costs, no matter what, before the financial crisis hit," according to Mr Balfour. "Low cost was the big phrase of the time," he said. "All our customers were saying 'China, China, China, we have got to get into China'. We were riding the wave and a few years later we found out the real cost the hard way."

He advises any company considering moving manufacturing or extending its supply chain abroad to take a "long, hard look at the costs and benefits". "We did a fairly rudimentary analysis," Mr Balfour said and two to three years later we found out the true cost the hard way."

Chapter 22: Is Reshoring Good Practice or Bad?

The Economist Magazine recently polled its online readers with the question, Do multinational corporations have a duty to maintain a strong presence in their home countries? 54% responded yes, and 46% no, proving that the issue is far from settled in our national debate.

The term reshoring refers to American and European corporations that have decided to bring some of their operations, and jobs, back to America and Europe. Several non-profit organizations and Government have taken up the cause of reshoring, and the debate over whether American and European corporations have a duty to bring some of their jobs home.

The non-profit group The Reshoring Initiative (reshorenow.org), shares our mission to bring good, well-paying manufacturing jobs back to the United States.

Last year marked the first time in decades that the USA did not lose jobs through offshoring, which is a good sign; but the work now begins to try and bring the millions of jobs that left our shores over the past 20 years. For example, in 2003, 150,000 factory-manufacturing jobs were outsourced overseas, while only 2,000 of the same jobs came back to the USA. This trend continued year after year during the 1990's and 2000's. Finally, and for several reasons, that trend has stopped.

The Reshoring Initiative founder Harry Moser effectively argues that it is in the best interest of the corporations, and its shareholders, to maintain a strong presence, and employ, manufacture and invest, in their country of origin.

One could argues that if American and European corporations properly factored in all of the costs of outsourcing, and not just the labour costs, then 25% of offshored jobs would come back to the USA and Europe with higher profitability.

There is an emerging consensus that the virtual workplace has its weaknesses, global collaboration has its limits and offshoring may have gone too far.

Wage and benefit increases of 15 to 20 percent per year at the average Chinese factory will slash China's labour-cost advantage over low-cost states in the U.S., from 55 percent today to 39 percent in 2016, when adjusted for the higher productivity of U.S. workers; because labour accounts for a small portion of a product's manufacturing costs, the savings gained from outsourcing to China will drop to single digits for many products.

Apple made a splash last December when it announced it would shift the manufacturing of one of its Macintosh computer products from China to the United States. Apple CEO Tim Cook said his company would invest $100 million to bring the manufacturing back to the U.S. this year. Concern about its reputation may have played some role in Apple's decision.

There are several reasons for U.S. and European corporations to bring our jobs home. The moral responsibility or duty, if any, to employ the same Americans or European that buy your products. The financial incentives, when you look at the entire economic reality of offshoring a company's operations overseas; and the public perception that may arise, of corporations taking advantage of the U.S. and European consumer without giving back in the form of jobs here at home.

Chapter 23: What to Consider When Reshoring

Almost everyone in any discrete product industry has heard these terms in the past three years as reports grow of companies bringing operations back to the United States and Europe or at least closer to a particular market region and the reassessment does not stop at manufacturing nor only American companies. Companies in North America and Europe are evaluating many operational activities, including engineering, manufacturing and service for the best location and situation (internal or outsourced). Changes in global economics, visibility of total costs of production, demand locations and customer preferences are most often cited as the drivers of this pendulum swing and, size or industry does not seem to be an indicator with companies from Apple, Nike, Whirlpool and Ford.

Indeed, we have seen a new set of companies like American Giant focusing solely on local sourcing and partnerships, selling the "made in..." as an integral part of the brand from design through marketing. American Giant has received a fair amount of hype from the fashion industry; however, the company has also garnered more serious consideration due to the exacting design process that is reflected all from sourcing through to manufacturing to create the greatest hoodie ever made.

Once the decision has been made to move or launch operations closer to home, the work begins and, while it might be tempting to think that it will all be easy with gains of similar culture, common languages and shorter time zone gaps, the same business discipline, planning and process adherence is needed and, there will be an adjustment phase; a training up period much like when you jump back into the pool for the first time in a decade.

Where do you start? You need the same discipline and focus that made offshoring successful for you; communication, dedicated resources, planning and clearly defined processes enforced by the critical business applications you already use or have identified as necessary. While you will be cutting costs in such areas as logistics charges, lower energy costs, volume commitments and improved quality (less scrap/rework), you will most likely have higher labour costs and potentially higher material costs. You will need to re-think some areas of the business. You might.

1. Consider product re-design for reduction in manufacturing process.

2. Investigate supplier options, ability to design with less materials or lower cost options or new technologies/efforts to reuse and reduce scrap or by-products.

3. Determine if automation opportunities exist as part of the transition.

4. For certain industries, the limited vertical ecosystem or supply chain, particularly in areas of tooling, may not only offset some of the cost savings, but continue the needs to support global process management across time zones and work cultures.

Don't assume that the benefits of bringing operations back home make the work any less challenging. Most of us have done this before – before business left the four walls or geographic boundaries. Your processes still need definition, application support and adherence. Communication, whether across the street or multiple time zones away, is still critical. Don't discard the discipline that made your offshoring successful. It is familiar, but still not easy.

A friend of ours once said "Reshoring, Made in America is like me back in the pool after years-long hiatus and it is hard and harder than I expected. I play tennis three to four times a week and regularly hit the gym or trails. I thought I was in fairly good shape, better than average; but, a few laps and my heart rate was in a zone that I believe medical professionals and trainers refer to as danger. I had to stop and rest. Breathing while swimming is a challenge at any time, but when you have been out of the water awhile, you can be an ultra distance runner and still suck wind."

"My efforts to re-engage with swimming sum up a truism that well applies to the organizational challenge of bringing some of the business back close; it is familiar, but not easy."

The data on comparative labour and energy costs may seem compelling but the process of bringing assembly work back to domestic factories from abroad is substantially more challenging than the economics alone would predict.

Rising labour costs in China and other emerging economies, high supply chain and logistics costs, and wide differentials in the costs for electricity and natural gas in different parts of the world are provoking a fresh round of relocation of manufacturing and production. While some labour-intensive jobs are moving out of China to Southeast Asia or the next emerging low-cost regions, some high-profile manufacturing work is returning to the United States and Western Europe, to the cheers of some who are proclaiming the beginnings of a manufacturing renaissance.

Wal-Mart holds supplier conferences to promote "Made in U.S.A.," and the retail giant encourages manufacturers to commit to producing in the United States by promising to purchase $50 billion more in U.S. manufactured goods in the next 10 years. It is targeting the reshoring of products made for its stores by trying to facilitate and accelerate reshoring efforts among its suppliers. Experts proclaim the re-emergence of the United States and Western Europe as a competitive place for manufacturing and are pushing their services with reshoring conferences, reports and lots of advice.

While the macroeconomic data on comparative labour and factor costs may be compelling, the actual process of reshoring; bringing assembly work back from abroad is hard work. This is especially true when the resources upon which a company draws (the supplier base, the workforce, and even the company's own internal product design capabilities) have atrophied.

The benefits were no surprise. Positioning manufacturing close to the market minimizes the inventory of goods in the pipeline and reduces delivery times. More importantly, the closeness reduces the length of ordering cycles, enabling companies to respond more quickly to market changes.

It was also no surprise that customers expect to pay little, if any, premium for products made domestically versus imported from abroad. Thus, it was important to pay a wage rate that was globally competitive when adjusted for productivity, and there can be no compromises on quality.

The challenges were less immediately apparent. Stabilizing the workforce, addressing organizational skills gaps, rethinking the capital/labour ratio, localizing the supply base and rethinking product design to leverage the proximity to manufacturing turned up consistently as important focus areas for managers.

In this chapter, I reflect on the experiences of these large reshoring projects and make recommendations for managers who are considering the United States or Western Europe as a location choice for new product-assembly operations. What is more, while most of the observations in this chapter are specific to reshoring in the United States, they contain insights that are relevant to markets and production around the globe.

Elevator maker has struggled with delays after relocating plant from Mexico to South Carolina. United Technologies found that bringing manufacturing jobs back to the U.S. can be a lot trickier than it sounds.

The company's move to relocate an Otis elevator plant from Mexico to South Carolina in late 2012 was hailed as a sign of a small renaissance in American manufacturing. The relocation was supposed to save money and help fill orders faster by putting the people who make new elevators next to the engineers who design them, and their customers. Now, it is clear the reality hasn't been so smooth. Production delays created a backlog of overdue elevators. Some customers cancelled their orders after being left waiting months, people in the elevator industry said. The plant Otis was leaving behind in Nogales, Mexico, had to stay open for half a year beyond its planned closing date to deal with the backlog.

The move became snarled in part because Otis added to its complexity by simultaneously reorganizing two other U.S. facilities and shrinking its product line, part of a broader plan to streamline its North American operations; but the company's experience also shows that with supply chains and skilled labour following American factories overseas in recent decades, coming home can be more complex than just deciding where to site a plant.

For Otis, it was an expensive lesson. The company has resolved the bulk of the problems and is working through the order backlog; but the delays cost United Technologies $60 million last year and it continue to weigh on earnings through the first half of 2014, the company said. "I think we failed on both the planning and the execution side," Robert McDonough, chief operating officer for the United Technologies unit that includes Otis, told analysts in March 2014.

Otis was founded in 1853 and is now the world's largest manufacturer, installer and servicer of elevators and escalators. It contributed about a quarter of the $2.6 billion in operating profit notched last year by United Technologies, which also makes Pratt & Whitney jet engines, Black Hawk helicopters and Carrier air conditioners.

When the elevator maker opened its new 423,000-square-foot facility in 2012 in a vacant Maytag factory in Florence, S.C., the company was a notable participant in a trend of "reshoring," where some companies reversed the movement of manufacturing work offshore to places like China. Multinationals like General Electric Co. and smaller industrial companies like Carlisle which makes construction materials, specialty tires and brakes, also brought work back to the U.S.

For some companies, the rise in Chinese wages as American hourly rates fell, along with the long transit, had made producing overseas less attractive.

For Otis, the return to the U.S. was supposed to herald a step up in efficiency. The company told The Wall Street Journal in the fall of 2011 that the relocation would lower the company's freight and logistics costs by 17%, and would cut costs a further 20% by having all of its white-collar elevator design and production workers on hand at the factory. The company says 70% of its customers in the U.S. and Canada are east of the Mississippi River, closer to the new plant than to Nogales.

Otis shipped its first elevator kits from Florence in the fall of 2012. The factory makes three varieties of elevators for low to mid rise apartment buildings, and construction of such developments was rebounding from the recession. The recovery drove Otis's orders up by double digits last year. The company's president, Pedro Baranda, told investors in March 2013 that the Florence facility was ramping up output to meet demand; but the facility couldn't keep up, leading to delays, executives told analysts in recent conference calls.

Otis executives first threw up a warning about the Florence project early last year. The company might need to hold off on closing down its Nogales factory, Otis told the bosses at United Technologies, because the new facility wasn't coming together as quickly as planned. The company now says it was trying to do too much at once. In addition to moving the plant,

Otis was busy cutting the number of products in its domestic business from seven to three. The company also was replacing the computer system that manages supply, manufacturing, shipping and financial information. Neither rollout went smoothly.

Adding to the complexity, Otis closed two other U.S. facilities, in Arizona and Indiana, and transferred the workers to South Carolina. The bigger hurdle, however, was putting together the necessary workforce.

"The challenge, I think, was moving your supply chain, with your factory and your engineering centre, all at once, and quite frankly to an area of the country where it's difficult to get enough trained workers," Greg Hayes, United Technologies' chief financial officer, said in an interview. "It's not like you are moving to Chicago or you are moving to Connecticut."

The reliance on Nogales dragged on longer than planned. At first, Otis executives wanted to postpone closing the Mexico plant from early spring until June 2013; but the number of delayed units continued to rise, hitting 1,000 in the middle of last year. The Mexican factory eventually remained open until September 2013.

"They just bit off more than they could chew, and again, shame on us," Mr. Hayes said. "The process didn't work in this case. Someone should have raised their hand and said, We are taking on more than we can handle at this time."

Otis overhauled the leadership of its North American operations this spring, bringing in Tom Vining, who had turned around the company's Chinese operations after a fatal accident involving an Otis escalator in Beijing.

By beefing up its field-installation teams, extending the life of its Mexican factory and hiring extra workers in Florence, Otis has managed to work down the backlog. This year, Otis expects new equipment sales in the Americas to grow by about 10%.

"There were customers that certainly felt the effect of some of the delays, and I think they would tell you that we have worked very closely with them to overcome some of the obstacles that some of the late deliveries caused," Mr. Vining said in an interview. "We made the investment and spent a lot of money to work with our customers."

The company wouldn't say how many customers cancelled orders, but spokeswoman Mary Milmoe said it wasn't a significant number. The costs of the Florence problems continue to pile up as much as $9 million in the first quarter, United Technologies said last month.

Officials in Florence are happy to have the company in town. The city of 37,000 in the Pee Dee region in South Carolina's north-eastern corner has a long industrial history. Officials said it has been trying to rebuild its manufacturing base.

Companies including Honda Motors Inc., to General Electric Co.'s medical device unit, and pharmaceutical giant Roche Holding AG have built or expanded factories in the region in recent years.

Otis now has 380 full-time employees in Florence, more than the 360 needed to claim a package of tax incentives from the county and state, as well as an additional 140 temporary workers. The jobs are higher skilled than the ones that sustained the area during the first manufacturing boom.

Stabilizing the Workforce

Establishing product-assembly operations means hiring people, often in large numbers. Appliance Park had a goal of hiring 2,500 new workers; the reshoring project in Fort Worth had the same target. Finding enough people with the right skills and finding them fast enough to support the ramp-up of operations was an enormous challenge. Appliance Park started with 10,000 applicants for an initial August 2012 job posting. Of the 6,142 who passed the initial screening, 730 were hired, but 228 were terminated in the first year (a 23% turnover rate). Fort Worth used six employment agencies to recruit job applicants, but the percentage of workers who first made it through the screening process and then continued past the first few days or weeks on the job to become a part of the regular workforce was depressingly low. "We brought them in on Monday, gave them initial training for two days and then put them out on the line Thursday for more training. By Friday, they were gone," recounted a manager in Fort Worth. Over the course of 10 weeks, the company had to hire 6,500 workers to yield the required 2,500 employees to begin volume production.

High worker turnover is a problem on the shop floor because it injects variability and unpredictability into production schedules. A factory cannot run a manufacturing line with consistent output and quality without a stable workforce. The same people need to come to work every day and run the production processes in a repeatable and consistent way. Constantly having to replace workers who drop out is not a path to success; the expenses associated with recruiting and training new employees when so many walk out the door are substantial.

I found that this problem had two main components; worker understanding and expectations of what a modern factory production job is, and management's ability to give workers reasons to stay. The first part reflects the great advances manufacturing processes have made in modern factories over the last two decades. Lean production systems, extensive use of measurement and information technology on the shop floor, and sophisticated quality systems have transformed the roles of frontline production and supply chain logistics workers. Yet worker perceptions of what manufacturing jobs entail have not kept pace. Many fresh recruits come to the job with inadequate preparation and an unrealistic view of what might be expected of them. "We hired people off the couch," remarked one plant manager.

Chapter 24: How to Ensure Your Reshoring Project Won't Fail

This is the kind of project that, done successfully, can add to the legacy a CEO leaves his company. Unfortunately, not all reshoring, onshoring and nearshoring projects are a success.

Consider Otis Elevator. case in earlier chapter of this book. Otis is one of many U.S. manufacturers, including GE, Whirlpool and NCR, which announced they were bringing factories back to the U.S. from China, Mexico and other countries and whose efforts did not go well.

You can avoid making the same mistakes Otis made and successfully reshore some of your production by considering these rules.

1. Request a business case to be written by the project team. This will help you understand the costs and justify the decision to the board.

2. Establish a disciplined project plan and assign an experienced project manager. If you don't have the resources, hire a consultant to help. Then monitor the progress.

3. Have a thorough analysis of the potential new location done, including an evaluation of the available talent pool. Partner with local community colleges

and universities to access or develop talent tailored to your specific needs.

4. Request a detailed evaluation of the costs associated with production. Can you reduce costs by introducing automation such as robotics and 3D printing? Are there government incentives that may tip the balance in favour of one location over another?

5. Plan out your supply base. Are your suppliers already in the U.S. or Western Europe, or will you have to re-establish new suppliers in these countries? This is not a trivial task and could take some time.

6. Even though your product may have been sold stateside previously, discuss with the team how you might localize it more for the U.S. market take advantage of this opportunity to update the product.

7. Have your CFO, or an outside expert, present to you and the board a report on the consequences of shutting down or reducing production in a foreign country. There may be hidden fines and penalties, as well as tax consequences.

8. Evaluate your global supply chain strategy. You may want to leave some production in growth markets such as China to address local and future global demand.

9. Assign a team member to document a road map in addition to the project plan. You need to see where the project is going and how it will end.

10. Maintain a close connection with the project manager and keep careful watch over the project. Play the role of devil's advocate and look for failure points.

11. Avoid biting off more than you and your staff can chew. It's better to make steady progress in this effort than to push for a quick launch.

More than half of U.S. and Western Europe based manufacturing executives at large companies report they are planning to bring production back home from China or are actively considering it. Some of these companies will be successful and others will struggle and fail. Reshoring takes careful consideration, planning and execution.

Following the steps in this chapter will help you avoid reshoring failure.

Chapter 25: Conclusion

Recently, rising energy prices, wage inflation and customer demand for shorter lead times have led many U.S. and Western European companies to consider "reshoring" the production of goods bound for domestic markets back to America and Western Europe.

As with all changes to a company's footprint, getting it right can be tricky. A decision to reshore should not be made absent the following considerations:

1. Focus on total costs instead of unit costs

Calculate indirect as well as direct expenses when evaluating offshore vs. onshore locations. Experts believe that by focusing on unit costs instead of the total cost of ownership which includes costs such as transportation, intellectual property risks and inventory carrying costs; manufacturers are overestimating potential savings from overseas operations by 20% to 30%.

2. Invest time to understand domestic labour markets

Supply, quality, and cost of labour are critical to the success of most (if not all) reshoring projects. Plant closures and an aging workforce have depleted the pool of skilled manufacturing workers in some parts of the country.

This shortage is further compounded by pressures to pursue a four-year college degree when a two-year technical degree may actually be more lucrative. Communities offering comprehensive, high quality technical training programs properly aligned with the needs of local employers are better equipped to deliver a pipeline of well-trained and highly-skilled workers.

3. Pursue government incentives to offset costs

Consistent with their long-standing support for projects that positively impact the overall economy, local, state, and federal governments have actively supported the resurgence of American manufacturing.

The U.S. Economic Development Administration's Make it in America Challenge is a $40 million initiative providing grants to support reshoring projects.

Many cities and states also offer financial and operating incentives (such as no or low-cost pre-employment training) to attract and support manufacturing operations; however, to realize maximum value, it is important to understand which programs are beneficial to your company's specific needs. Of course, incentives are only part of the equation and should never be allowed to drive a project to a location that doesn't meet the company's operating requirements.

4. Analyze transportation cost differentials

In and out-bound transportation costs, including the delivery of raw materials and the shipment of finished product, can comprise a major share of the cost of goods sold in the U.S., and can vary widely depending on the location. Given shortages of truck drivers and equipment, as well as trends towards sustainability, it may also be prudent to investigate alternative modes of transportation, such as rail.

5. Carefully assess product demand

Spurred by efforts such as Walmart's $250 billion "Buy American" campaign, locally produced goods are in high demand. However, miscalculations can lead to lost investment and time. In 2010, Stanley Furniture announced it would relocate production of baby cribs from China to Robbinsville, N.C. The new cribs were marketed under the Young America brand, a new line of high quality youth furniture. After investing $10 million in new state-of-the-art equipment, sales failed to meet expectations and the company is closing the facility.

6. Diligently review utility services and rates

Reliable, cost-competitive electric power is critical for many manufacturing operations. Power prices can vary from (occasionally) below 4¢ to above 12¢ per kWh; a delta of millions of dollars annually for large users. For operations such as food processing, water quality and availability and wastewater treatment capacity are also key. Again, rates and available capacities will vary greatly between locations and even among sites in the same location.

7. Consider tax climates

State and local tax rates and structures vary greatly across the country. Carefully assess the potential impact of corporate income taxes and taxes on the purchase of production equipment, real estate, machinery, and inventory. It is critical to consider company accounting structures and strategies to find the optimal arrangement for the specific operation.

In short, deciding whether and or where to reshore a manufacturing operation in the U.S. or Western Europe is a complex decision involving a multitude of considerations. Companies can minimize risks and reap rewards by carefully analyzing these factors.

Good luck !!

www.ingramcontent.com/pod-product-compliance
Lightning Source LLC
Chambersburg PA
CBHW051535170526
45165CB00002B/745